The Stationers' Voice

The English Almanac Trade in the Early Eighteenth Century

TRANSACTIONS
of the
AMERICAN PHILOSOPHICAL SOCIETY
Held at Philadelphia
For Promoting Useful Knowledge
Volume 95, Part 4

The Stationers' Voice

☙❧

The English Almanac Trade in the Early Eighteenth Century

Timothy Feist

American Philosophical Society
Philadelphia • 2005

Copyright © 2005 by the American Philosophical Society for its *Transaction* series. All rights reserved.

ISBN-10: 0-87169-954-0
ISBN-13: 978-0-87169-954-1
US ISSN: 0065-9746

Library of Congress Cataloging-in Publication Data

Feist, Timothy, 1975–
    The stationers' voice : the English almanac trade in the early eighteenth century / Timothy Feist.
        p. cm. — (Transactions of the American Philosophical Society, ISSN 0065-9746 ; v. 95, pt. 4)
    Includes bibliographical references and index.
    ISBN-13: 978-0-87169-954-1 (pbk.)
        1. Almanacs, English—History—18th century. 2. Stationers' Company (London, England) 3. Book industries and trade—England—London—History—18th century. 4. Publishers and publishing—England—History—18th century. 5. Authors and publishers—England—History—18th century. 6. Popular literature—England—History and criticism. 7. Popular culture—England—History—18th century. 8. England—Intellectual life—18th century. 9. England—Social life and customs—18th century. 10. Great Britain—Commerce—History—18th century. I. Title. II. Series.

AY33.F45 2005
031.02—dc22

2005048118

Contents

Acknowledgments

I have never met Robin Myers, but her work in editing and micro-filming the Stationers' Company archives was the prerequisite for this monograph. The project itself originated in Professor Lance Bertelsen's seminar on eighteenth-century British literature and popular culture at the University of Texas at Austin. It grew into a Master's thesis in the Department of History under the direction of Associate Professor Neil Kamil (Professor Brian Levack served as secondary reader for the thesis). The staffs of the Harry Ransom Humanities Research Center and the Perry Castaneda Library facilitated my research with tireless efficiency.

As an active-duty Marine officer, I owe particularly good language to my Corps for sending me to Austin, and to my fellow Marines for enduring much hazard and hardship while I studied in comfort. I offer quite similar admiration and thanks to my wife, Rhonda Reneé.

⧼ Chapter One ⧽

Introduction

" Where Men are under an unlimited Allowance to publish their Sentiments of things, it's the Publick Establishment, that must suffer the sharpest attack."[1] When Daniel Defoe made this argument in 1699,[2] he had the Worshipful Company of Stationers in mind. It was, after all, stationers—individual printers and booksellers—who were instigating that chaotic jumble of political, scientific, and theological ideas which worried the young polemicist. But it was also the stationers as a community—the Stationers' Company—which exemplified quite the opposite possibility, the self-restraint and ideological decorum that could result when public and private interests merged. No single item embodied this cultural alchemy more completely than the English almanac, simultaneously an emblem of bumptious popular culture and the official product of the Company of Stationers.

Historians typically think of the seventeenth century as the golden age for English almanacs, and—if astrological ingenuity is the standard—this is a valid judgment. In commercial terms, however, the genre's true heyday arrived with the eighteenth century. The Stationers' Company possessed a royal monopoly on the entire almanac trade, and—despite the variety of titles—by the early eighteenth century, almanacs did not reflect the views of numerous individual compilers but of this single corporate author. Almanacs were first and foremost a commodity, and one has to consider them as products before one can interpret them intelligently as literature.

Such a project requires us to account for both the logic of the market and the logic of the Stationers' Company—its hierarchy, methods of internal regulation, patronage practices, and self-defined interests. The market logic of consumer appeal dictated that content should reflect the current interests and understandings of a majority of English consumers. A spectacular volume of sales and comfortable profits throughout the eighteenth century confirmed this logic, marking the almanac as an accurate literary snapshot of the cultural mainstream at its time of production. At the same time, the political logic of monopoly circumscribed this reflective tendency. It dictated that eighteenth century almanacs would contain a uniform message, one geared to burnish the Stationers' Company's corporate image and to foster the sort of society the Company preferred. The almanacs' message was widely disseminated and widely consumed, but—regardless of its popularity—it was shaped by the idiosyncratic motives of the Stationers' Company. These conclusions carry implications for a variety of questions relevant to eighteenth century studies including authorship, consumerism, corporate development, national identity, scientific worldviews, and political attitudes.

Almanac Artifacts: A Note in Sources & Structure

It will be noted that this paper concerns itself with an extremely narrow sample of almanacs, those produced in 1711 (for the year 1712). In addition, while the paper purports to confine itself to the early eighteenth century, many portions of the argument (particularly in the chapters on production, authorship and patronage) trace patterns which extend well beyond that period. These apparent eccentricities result from the two distinct (yet interrelated) lines of inquiry that I have pursued in my investigation of the almanac trade.

An analysis of production is necessarily centered on products. Accordingly, this paper asks how a particular group of literary artifacts came to exist in their particular form, containing their particular texts, at a particular moment in time. It happens that the artifacts I use are located at the Humanities Research Center at the University of Texas at Austin. The HRC owns only a smattering of eighteenth century almanacs, but the vagaries of collection purchasing have left the HRC with all (save one) of the book almanacs published by the Stationers' Company in 1711. This narrow sample of artifacts provides a material hub around which to construct a larger historical inquiry into almanac publication. Almanacs from any other year in the early eighteenth century could conceivably have served this purpose, but the HRC's 1711 sample is particularly useful since Parliament passed a Stamp Act in that year just in time to raise the price of almanac production by two pence per copy. This disruption in the normal production process was a particularly revealing moment, and it carried significant long- and short-term implications for almanac production in England. At any rate, the eighteen almanacs that form the material touchstone of this study include:

- *Great News from the Stars: or, an Ephemeris for the Year 1712.* by William Andrews.
- *Merlinus Anglicanus Junior: or, the Starry Messenger for the Year of Human Redemption, 1712* by Henry Coley.
- *Culpepper Revived. Being an Almanack for the Year of our Blessed Saviour's Incarnation 1712* by Nathaniel Culpepper.
- *Speculum Uranicum* . . . by Thomas Fowles.
- *Astrologus Britannicus* . . . Richard Gibson.
- *Fly.* An Almanack For the Year of our Lord God 1712.
- *Swallow* . . . by John Swallow.
- *Vox Stellarum* . . . by Francis Moore.[4]
- *Perkins. A New Almanack* . . . by Francis Perkins.
- *Rose 1712. A New Almanack* . . . by George Rose.
- *Apollo Anglicanus: The English Apollo* . . . by Richard Saunders.
- *Angelus Britannicus* . . . by John Tanner.
- *Great Britain's Diary: or, the Union-Almanack* . . . by John Tipper.
- *Calendarium Astrologicum.* . . by Thomas Trigge.
- *White, 1712* . . . by Thomas White.
- *Olympia Domata* . . . by John Wing.[5]
- *Poor Robin. 1712. An Almanack of the Old and New Fashion: or, An Ephemeris in Jest and Earnest* . . .
- *Woodhouse, A Prognostication* . . . by John Woodhouse.[6]

This sample encompasses all of the book almanac titles printed by the Stationers Company in 1711 except for one, John Tipper's *Ladies' Diary*.

Interpreting and explaining these artifacts requires a sharp focus on the people—Stationer leadership, compilers and printers—who participated in their production. At the same time, however, one cannot understand the relationships between these people unless they are placed in the context of large patterns in the production process. Thus, chapters on production tend to oscillate between trends spanning the entire Stationer monopoly and events and information specific to the situation in 1711. An analysis of a particular moment in the early eighteenth century involves contextual evidence spanning much of the early modern era.

The structure of the paper follows a similar pattern, establishing general conditions of production and patterns of relationship in the almanac trade and culminating with a detailed interpretation of almanacs produced in 1711. These artifacts serve as narrative focal point and analytical touchstone, but the primary purpose of this paper is not to interpret almanac content. The purpose is to explore almanac production during an era hitherto portrayed in teleological terms as a decline. This analysis presupposes that eighteenth century almanacs ought to be considered as commodities shaped by the specific conditions of their production before they are used as historical evidence. A brief interpretive exercise in chapter seven uses the HRC sample to demonstrate the potential significance of this approach and to explore some of its implications for our understanding of the British past. Yet because this interpretation concerns such a limited sample, I am at pains to emphasize that its observations are technically only valid (provided they are valid at all) for 1711, possibly for years immediately before and after, probably not for the entire eighteenth century. My interpretive foray is consciously suggestive rather than exhaustive. If this paper indicates some of the ways in which awareness of almanac trade might inform historical evaluation of almanac content, extensive, systematic interpretation along these lines remains to be done.

Notes

1. Daniel Defoe, "A Letter to a Member of Parliament, Shewing the Necessity of Regulating the Press," in *Freedom of the Press: Six Tracts 1698–1709* (New York: Garland Publishing, 1974), 34.

2. When citing dates in this paper, I take the year to have begun on 1 January. When quoting contemporary sources, I have retained the original spelling and capitalization. I have ignored original italicization, and modified punctuation occasionally in the interest of clarity.

3. For a contrary argument based on the astrological content of a single title, see Paul D. Wiggins, "Moore's Almanac and Eighteenth-Century Astrology" (Ph.D. diss., University of London, 2003).

4. The HRC's copy of this almanac is a pirated version composed of a false "Poor Robin" title page attached to the body of *Vox Stellarum*.

5. The HRC lists *Olympia Domata's* ephemeris as a second, separate almanac by John Wing: "*Wing. A Prognostication, For the Year of our Lord God, 1712.*" References to *Olympia Domata* in this paper should be taken to compass both the work listed under that title, and the work listed as "*Wing.*"

6. As the title suggests, this artifact consists only of the *Woodhouse* almanac's prognostication section.

❧ Chapter Two ❧

The Stationers' Company

The Worshipful Company of Stationers was the London guild of merchants and artisans associated with the printing trade. Its members included printers, bookbinders, type-founders, engravers, paper-makers, and booksellers. It was unique among English guilds because while it performed the normal functions of a trade association by regulating trade practices, providing charity to impoverished members, and so forth, it also functioned as a commercial concern in its own right. The Company's legal, commercial, and political dominance of the printing industry made it a pervasive influence in early modern English literature.[1]

Membership and Hierarchy

Readers should envision relationships between stationers in the physical context of Stationers' Hall, a complex of substantial brick buildings at the corner of Ave Maria Lane and Paternoster Row just north of St. Martin's of Ludgate Church in London. This acre of ground on Ludgate Hill contained two rows of houses let to tenants, as well as an imposing Hall set behind iron gates where the Company held its meetings and functions. The Hall was the epicenter of English publishing, "a point of passage, rendezvous, and negotiation for all members of the book trade." Despite the absence of battlements and moats, Adrian Johns's characterization of the Hall as "a castle" seems particularly apt; with its secluded centrality, the Hall made an appropriate setting for the highly structured society of its denizens.[2]

One could acquire membership in the Company of Stationers by four different means—service, patrimony, redemption, or translation. As with other London guilds, acquiring the freedom of the Company was synonymous with receiving the freedom of the City, and the customs of the City governed Company policy on apprenticeship and freedom. At the same time it should be noted that by the early eighteenth century, a tradesman could conduct business quite freely in London without joining any guild at all. Company membership offered certain advantages, but it had ceased to be a legal prerequisite for trade.

Freedom by "service" meant that an individual completed an agreed period of indenture—as apprentice to a master member of the Company; by the 1700s, term length had been standardized at seven years. At the end of an indenture, a master presented his apprentice before the Company's ruling body, the Court, and the Court officially bestowed membership—or "freedom"—on the apprentice. "Patrimony" offered a shortcut to this process. Any member of the Company had the right to present his or her children for the Company's freedom without first indenting them. On both occasions, whether freeing someone by service or patrimony, the master (usually, although sometimes the apprentice's family) paid a 3s. 4d. fine to the Company.[3] Stationers learning their trade abroad or through apprenticeship to a nonmember could enter the Company by "redemption" or "purchase." Such would-be freemen paid negotiated fines averaging around £5. More rarely, some members were "translated" from another guild at their own request, pending the consent of both the losing and gaining guilds. Negotiations determined the fines paid to both companies, as well as the translated member's relative seniority in his new company.[4]

Freeing by redemption and translation appear to have caused resentment, especially among printers. In his biographical list of printers, John Dunton described some of his subjects as being "bred a printer" because they had served apprenticeships under reputable masters.[5] Similarly, Samuel Negus—himself a printer freed by service—disparaged those "who never have been brought up to that business, and ought to be put down."[6] Where Dunton implied a higher level of professional competence among those bred to the trade, Negus asserted that upstart printers were more likely to print seditious or troublesome literature. Both statements smack of special pleading, but it is not hard to imagine veterans who had earned their place the hard way viewing redemption as illegitimate, a cheap shortcut around honest effort. All freemen were officially equal, but this could not have prevented tacit social distinctions among freemen coming from different professional backgrounds.

Informal divisions aside, an official hierarchy of status and position governed the legal and ceremonial life of the guild. A freeman of the Stationers' Company could experience three levels of corporate status in his lifetime. All freemen entered the Company as part of the yeomanry, the guild's general population. Yeomen agreed to pay quarterly dues (cleverly titled the "Quarteridge") and to abide by company rules, which included the obligation to contribute against any legal assessments laid on the Company, not to abuse other members, and not to betray the Company's secrets or conspire against it. A stationer might progress from journeyman to master and still spend his entire life as a yeoman.[7] Women, it seems, could never expect any other status. By custom, widows of London freemen inherited their dead husbands' freedom and retained it for life, and women acquired freedom independently by both patrimony and service. Apprenticeship records indicate that women regularly became masters in each of the stationers' trades. They owned and managed shops; took, trained, and freed apprentices; and generally conducted business on a daily basis like any other tradesman. But they could not become a liveryman or an assistant in the Company of Stationers.[8]

If the yeomanry comprised the Company's House of Commons, the livery and assistants were its Lords and Cabinet. "Putting on the livery" literally meant representing the Company at ceremonial occasions by wearing the Stationers' distinctive gown and hood, but it implied a variety of privileges as well. Liverymen were eligibile for larger shares of the English Stock (a term explained below), Renter Warden positions, further advancement, participation in annual ceremonies such as the Lord Mayor's Day procession, and attendance at quarterly dinners given by senior members of the Court.[9] By the eighteenth century, it was tacitly assumed that only masters merited livery status, but merely owning one's own business was in itself insufficient to merit election.

Livery status also implied comfortable wealth. When the Court of Assistants "called" a man to be "clothed," it assessed a £20 fine, plus 15s. in fees to Company functionaries. The call was not an optional invitation but a legal order; a refusal to be clothed doubled the fine. Imposing such an injunction on a poor master could put him in a serious financial quandary, so the Court considered this carefully before it extended the call to a yeomen. A successful refusal of the call required legal action and incurred considerable social opprobrium, as in the case of John Salisbury—who became known as "a desperate Hypergorgonick Welchman" after suing the Company to avoid taking the livery.[10] Nor was such vitriol mere pique. High status in the Stationers' Company carried significant, sometimes onerous, administrative and financial obligations. The rejection of the livery was in some respects tantamount to selfishness.

The only titled livery positions were Renter Warden and Assistant Renter Warden. The Court of Assistants appointed liverymen to these positions in order of seniority. An electee could serve in the office by collecting quarteridge from members and rent from Company tenants, or he could decline service and pay a fine of £24 instead, which officially counted as service. The Renter Wardens had to provide dinner for their fellow liverymen on the Lord Mayor's Day, which was a hefty obligation by the early eighteenth century when the number of liverymen exceeded two hundred. Renter Wardens served for one year only, and it became a prerequisite for one to serve (or fine) as Renter Warden for assistant status eligibility, the third and most exclusive level in the Company hierarchy.[11]

The Court of Assistants was the stationers' oligarchy, which decided Company policy, enjoyed most of its privileges, and incurred its heaviest responsibilities. Like most oligarchies, the Court was a self-perpetuating body with the power to select and regulate its own members. Company bylaws set no limit on the number of assistants, but membership for the decades before and after 1711 appears to have averaged about twenty. Seniority was important but not decisive in determining who was considered for assistantship, and the Court exercised considerable discretion in its elections.[12] The significant costs demanded of Renter Wardens probably accounted for the mere 15s. fine that new assistants paid upon election. Anyone elected to the Court was already a wealthy man and was able to bear the financial obligations of leadership status.

Most of those costs were incurred during service on the Court's three-man executive committee, which consisted of a Master, an Upper Warden, and an Under Warden. Serving or fining for two terms as Upper or Lower Warden was required before one became eligible for Master. Fines for refusing to serve were set at the Court's pleasure but usually ranged from £10 to £20 for Master, £12 to £24 for the first time as Upper Warden (£6 for a second term), and £10 to £20 for Under Warden (£5 for a second term). Additionally, senior assistants who had served their two Wardenships had to pay similar amounts to retain seniority every time a junior assistant was elected to the Master's chair ahead of them.[13] The Court elected its Master and Wardens annually, but it imposed no term limits so the same man could—and often did—serve multiple consecutive terms. The Court selected these officers by voting on nominees. Ties—and there were many—normally went "into the box" so that officers were often elected by lot rather than by vote.[14] Upon election, the Wardens and Master were obligated to provide a venison dinner for the entire livery. Also, the assistants occasionally took up charitable collections among themselves to aid stationers in need of emergency assistance.[15] In return for these financial outlays, assistants received social prestige, eligibility for an assistant's share of the English Stock, and power over the Company's patronage. If nothing else can be known, it is markedly clear that the path to official prominence in the Stationers' Company was paved with gold.[16]

Yet service on the Court demanded more than just money; it exacted a considerable amount of the assistants' time as well. Aside from a regular Court meeting held at 10:00 a.m. on the first Monday of every month, assistants had to appear at emergency sessions called by the Master, which were sometimes distressingly frequent. Committees of assistants conducted trade negotiations, initiated and supervised prosecutions, lobbied Parliament, wrote advertisements, and reviewed Company account books. Additionally, preparation for and participation in every Company ceremony was mandatory for the leadership. The variety and number of their obligations gives one the impression that the assistants worked rather hard for their perks.

Ceremonial Rhythm

As a community, the Stationers' Company defined itself by its annual cycle of official ceremony. These rituals communicated the Company's place in the larger society and reinforced the individual stationer's identity within the guild. The Company's year began in early July—the "Saturday after St. Peters Day"—with the election of a new Master and Wardens by the assistants and Renter Wardens. A month later in early August, the new Wardens treated the Court and livery to an Election Feast, also called the "Venison Feast" after its traditional main dish. The Court and livery met at Stationers' Hall at 10:00 a.m., proceeded next door to St. Martin's of Ludgate Church, and then marched back to the Hall after the service for dinner. The chaplains of the Archbishop of Canterbury and the Bishop of London were "solemnly invited" to the Election Feast every year. In early November, the livery accompanied the Lord Mayor to Westminster in their barge as part of the annual Lord Mayor's Day procession. They met at the waterfront at 9:00 a.m. and concluded the day with the Renter Wardens' dinner at the Hall. On 26 March the Court met to elect (or reelect) the Renter Wardens, as well as the Company's functionaries: Clerk, Beadle, Barge-Master, and Barge-Master's Mate. On Ash Wednesday, the Court and livery proceeded from the Hall to St. Austin's Church for a sermon and then back to the Hall for

"Cakes and Ale" provided at Company expense. The City required the Court and livery's presence at the Guildhall on 24 June and 29 September to elect the Sheriffs and Lord Mayor, respectively. Monthly Courts, or meetings of the assistants and Renter Wardens, occurred at 10:00 a.m. on the first Tuesday of every month except in January; assistants were expected to attend in livery. As demonstrated below, other ceremonies associated with English Stock government, with publication, and with Company charity supplemented these political rituals. Taken together, the repetition and predictability of these ceremonies reinforced the Company's commitment to association and gave structure to their communal life. In symbol as in substance, the stationers' community marked time together.[17]

Commercial Purpose: The English Stock

Its function as a commercial enterprise distinguished the Stationers' Company from other guilds. The Company's "English Stock" was the only corporation in England legally authorized to produce and wholesale certain categories of popular books—primarily schoolbooks, psalters, and almanacs. While the Company enjoyed other "patents" (or royal monopolies) on Latin, Irish, and Scottish titles from time to time, it was the English patent granted by James I in 1603 that proved to be the Company's gold mine, a source of significant commercial and political power for nearly two centuries. King James had intended the monopoly to provide £200 yearly for the Company's poor, but the Stock produced profits far above this amount, and the excess benefited shareholders rather than the poor. To raise capital, the Court allotted shares of decreasing value and increasing number to the three classes of stationers: fifteen assistant shares worth £320 each, thirty livery shares worth £160 each, and sixty yeoman shares worth £80 each. The Court of Assistants decided annually on a proper rate of return, and "Dividend Day"—which lasted from 10:00 a.m. to 1:00 p.m. on a designated day in December—quickly became part of the Company's annual ceremonial cycle. So did the Court's meeting to elect six Stock-Keepers—the Stock's equivalent of a Board of Trustees—every 1 March.[18]

Because dividends usually came in at 12.5 percent, demand for shares inevitably exceeded supply. By 1711, the Company's members had grown so numerous—and shareholders were living so long—that the Court had long since expanded the Stock to include at least two dozen half-yeoman shares. Actual yeomen had been squeezed out of the Stock altogether; most assistants held livery shares, and nearly all of the yeoman and half-yeoman shares belonged to liverymen. From the outset, the Court zealously guarded against any possibility of outside takeover or control. Shareholders could own only one share at a time, and they could not mortgage their share in any way. They and their widows retained their shares for life, after which the shares reverted to the Stock, and the Court itself selected new owners. Not surprisingly, the assistants usually voted one of their own number into the vacated share if it was worth more than his own. The lucky recipient gave up his old share in turn, and paid the value of the new share into the Stock treasury. This caused a ripple effect that injected more capital into the Stock as junior stationers moved into shares progressively vacated by their seniors.[19]

The daily business of the Stock fell to the Warehouse-Keeper, (or "Treasurer"), a salaried agent who managed the production, storage, and sale of Stock books from the Stock Warehouse in the basement of Stationers' Hall.[20] The shareholders of the Stock met annually in March and elected a board of six Stock-Keepers—two from each of the three share categories—to supervise the Stock during the subsequent year. The full Stock Board included the Master and Wardens, so that the Court of Assistants dominated the English Stock to the same extent as it dominated the Company at large. In practice, the Court and the Stock Board were synonymous.[21]

Notes

1. Although this paper considers the Stationers' Company in terms of authorship, it touches on themes of business history which merit further development. Such a study might begin by attempting to situate the Stationers' Company on the organizational scale proposed in Naomi Lamoreaux, Daniel M. G. Raff, and Peter Temin, "Beyond Markets and Hierarchies: Toward a New Synthesis of American Business History," *American Historical Review* 108, 2 (2003), 404–33. It could build on the conclusions of this paper by examining the Company both as an agent within British society and as an agent *of* society. The latter notion was articulated in Stephen B. Adams, "Review of *Coordination and Information: Historical Perspectives on the Organization of Enterprise*," Naomi Lamoreaux & Daniel Raff, *Journal of Interdisciplinary History* 27, 3 (Winter 1997), 502–4.

2. Cyprian Blagden, *The Stationers' Company: A History 1403–1959* (Cambridge, MA: Harvard University Press, 1960), 215–22. Adrian Johns, *The Nature of the Book: Print and Knowledge in the Making* (Chicago: University of Chicago Press, 1998), 190–200; Ann Saunders, "The Stationers' Hall," in *The Stationers' Company and the Book Trade*, ed. Robin Myers and Michael Harris (New Castle, DE: Oak Knoll Press, 1997), 1–10.

3. English monetary denominations during the eighteenth century and before were derived from the Latin names for analogous Roman denominations. Pounds sterling were denoted by a lower-case "l" for the Roman *librae*, shillings with an "s" for *solidi*, pence with a "d" for *denarii*, and half-pennies with a q for *quadrantes*. In this paper, I will use the modern symbol £ for pounds sterling, "s" for shillings, and "d" for pence. Half-pennies, God bless them, will be rounded to the nearest penny. John Tipper, *Great Britain's Diary: or, The Union-Almanack for the Year of Our Lord 1712* (London: Company of Stationers, 1711).

4. Blagden, *Stationers' Company: A History*, 34–35, 162, 181–82. Also see the very helpful glossary section in Robin Myers, *The Stationers' Company Archive; an Account of the Records 1554–1984* (Detroit: Omnigraphics, 1990).

5. John Nichols, *Literary Anecdotes of the Eighteenth Century Comprizing Biographical Memoirs of William Bowyer, Printer, F.S.A. and Many of His Learned Friends; an Incidental View of the Progress and Advancement of Literature in This Kingdom during the Last Century; and Biographical Anecdotes of a Considerable Number of Eminent Writers and Ingenious Artists; with a Very Copious Index* (London: Nichols, Son, and Bentley, 1812), 1: 73.

6. Samuel Negus, "A Compleat and Private List of All the Printing-Houses in and about the Cities of London and Westminster, Together with the Printers' Names, What News-Papers They Print, and Where They Are to Be Found: Also an Account of the Printing-Houses in the Several Corporation Towns in England; Most Humbly Laid before the Right Honourable the Lord Viscount Townshend," quoted in John Nichols, *Literary Anecdotes*, vol. 1 (London: Nichols, Son, and Bentley, 1812), 289.

7. Blagden, *Stationers' Company: A History*, 35, 156, 162.

8. A casual glance through the "Master and Apprentice Calendar for 6 April 1687 to 5 May 1707" reveals an extensive female presence in the printing trade: Elizabeth Anson, Elizabeth Ashley, Susanna Battersby, Rebecca Bonwick, Elizabeth Hodgkinson, Elizabeth Mallott (widow of David), Ann Maxwell, Ann Norris, Anne Mott, Ann Noodham, Katherine Maddocks (widow of Thomas), Anne Purslow, Jane Rayment (widow of William), "widdow Susan Slater," Susan Streat, "Widd Hannah Sink," Hanna Sawridge (widow of George Sawbridge), Mary Thompson, Mary Tanson (widow of Richard), and Margaret White. Female apprentices included: Mary Hoult, Mary Wingfeild (to Ann Noodham), Barbara Hubbard, Ann Quill, Elizabeth Hammond, Margrett Hobb, Elizabeth Road, Dorothy Peake, Dorothy Grabham, Elizabeth Robins (to Elizabeth Anson), Rebecca Brimsriead (to Elizabeth Ashley), and Elizabeth Chamberlain. Unless otherwise noted, all female apprentices were bound to male printers, and the majority of female masters took male apprentices. The Stationers' archive contains a considerable amount of incidental evidence pertaining to women's participation in the London printing and bookselling trades, and any scholar in-

vestigating women's status or activities in early modern England ought to consult it. Worshipful Company of Stationers, "Master and Apprentice Calendars," in *Records of the Worshipful Company of Stationers 1554–1920*, ed. Robin Myers, (Cambridge: Chadwyck-Healey, 1985) 37.

9. Blagden, *Stationers' Company: A History*, 115, 158–59, 230.

10. The Beadle assisted in this decision making process, despite his functionary status. According to a list of "Rules for the Beadle" composed in 1780, he was officially obligated to keep track of "Names of such Persons as are proper to be called on the Livery." Worshipful Company of Stationers, "Series 1—Box M: English Stock and Irish Plantation (Manor of Pellipar) 1673–1964," in *Records of the Worshipful Company of Stationers 1554–1920*, ed. Robin Myers (Cambridge: Chadwyck-Healey, 1985), 104, Folder 6. The emphasis on propriety rather than seniority is telling. The Court normally enforced its call. For example, on 1 May 1710 Edward Castle refused to "take the Clothing of this Company upon him. Thereupon 'twas Ordered and resolved by the Court to Insist upon their former Orders and that he be proceeded against upon with his refusal." Worshipful Company of Stationers, "Court Book G; Fair Copy of Court Minutes 8 November 1697 to 6 May 1717," in *Records of the Worshipful Company of Stationers 1554–1920*, ed. Robin Myers (Cambridge: Chadwyck-Healey, 1985) 57. Salisbury quote is in John Dunton, *The Life and Errors of John Dunton Late Citizen of London; Written by Himself in Solitude. With an Idea of a New Life; Wherein Is Shewn How He'd Think, Speak, and Act, Might He Live over His Days Again: Intermix'd with the New Discoveries the Author Has Made in His Travels Abroad, and in His Private Conversation at Home. Together with the Lives and Characters of a Thousand Persons Now Living in London, &C.* (London: S. Malthus, 1705), 287.

11. Cyprian Blagden, "The Stationers' Company in the Eighteenth Century," *Guildhall Miscellany* 10 (1959): 42–43; Blagden, *Stationers' Company: A History*, 159–60.

12. On 4 June 1705, "The Court proceeded to the Eleccion of Fower New Assistants and the severall psons according to their standings were putt down in writing and scored for." From this, one deduces that the Court had the power to decide when to hold and to determine how many new members to accept. Using the nebulous term "standing" rather than seniority is significant in this case. The Court minutes often refer to "seniority," but when it came to selecting assistants, more categories came under consideration. Stationers, "Court Book G; Fair Copy of Court Minutes 8 November 1697 to 6 May 1717," 57.

13. For example, on 3 July 1710 when Churchill fined out of Master, Captain Roycroft "moved that in regard the Court had Chose Mr. Churchill Master who was his junior that the Court would Admitt him to the usuall fine for Master to preserve his Seniorityship" and was permitted to do so. At the next Court meeting on 7 August 1710, almanac printer Thomas Hodgkin also "moved that in as much as Mr. Churchill who was his Junior was Chosen

Master he Desired to be admitted to the usuall fine for his 2d Year upper Warden and for Master to preserve his Seniorityship." Mr. Clarke did the same. Ibid.

14. For example, see the election held on 6 July 1702. Ibid.

15. For example, on 3 May 1703 the assistants "voluntarily subscribed" £10 8s. to assist the son of their recently deceased Beadle. Ibid.

16. Blagden, *Stationers' Company: A History,* 38, 156–58.

17. See "The Business of the Beadle of the Stationers Company" for a detailed description of the Company's ceremonies. Stationers, "Series 1—Box M: English Stock and Irish Plantation (Manor of Pellipar) 1673–1964," 104, Folder 6. See also Blagden, *Stationers' Company: A History,* 156, 159, 250–51; Johns, *Nature of the Book,* 210–12; Myers, 3–12.

18. Specific times are taken from a Beadle's announcement preserved in Stationers, "Series 1—Box M: English Stock and Irish Plantation (Manor of Pellipar) 1673–1964," 104, Folder 11.

19. For an example of the ripple effect, look at the disposition of Margaret Royston's £320 share on 18 December 1702. On word of her death, the Court voted her share to Assistant William Rawlins. His £160 livery share went to Assistant Samuel Sprint whose £80 yeoman share went to a mere liveryman, Henry Bonwick. The total capital paid into the Stock during this process amounted to a tidy £560. Stationers, "Court Book G; Fair Copy of Court Minutes 8 November 1697 to 6 May 1717." For references on the general structure of the Stock and the allocation of shares, see Cyprian Blagden, "The English Stock of the Stationers' Company: An Account of Its Origins," *The Library* 10 (1955), 163–85; Cyprian Blagden, "The English Stock of the Stationers' Company in the Time of the Stuarts," *The Library* 12 (1957), 167–86; Blagden, "The Stationers' Company in the Eighteenth Century," 41; Blagden, *Stationers' Company: A History,* 92–97, 230, 242–45. A useful snapshot of the politics surrounding the Stock's profits, dividends, and charitable distributions can be found in a Chancery Brief dated 4 November 1742 in Worshipful Company of Stationers, "Series 2—Box 33: Legal Papers (1680–1893)," in *Records of the Worshipful Company of Stationers 1554–1920,* ed. Robin Myers (Cambridge: Chadwyck-Healey, 1985) 112.

20. For a detailed look at the Warehouse-Keeper's routine, his privileges and obligations, see the "Rules Orders and Instructions for the . . . Treasurer or Warehouse keeper of the Stock of this Company" for 1780 in Stationers, "Series 1—Box M: English Stock and Irish Plantation (Manor of Pellipar) 1673–1964," 104, Folder 6.

21. Blagden, "The Stationers' Company in the Eighteenth Century," 44–45.

᧭ Chapter Three ᧨

Almanacs

*T*he almanac trade involved three categories of almanac, each produced in staggering quantities throughout the eighteenth century. This mass production occurred in a predictable and profitable annual cycle, making the Stationers' Company an early exemplar of something like industrial capitalism. The sheer volume of this trade leads one to conclude that the cultural influence of almanacs must have been significant.

Almanac Taxonomy

Legally, "almanac" in eighteenth century England was another name for a calendar.[1] A printed tool used chiefly for marking the passage of time, utility defined the almanac genre so that, in common usage, the term came to signify not just a calendar but a compendium of information useful for orienting one's life to the annual rhythms of commerce, government, and the physical world. The Stationers' Company—sole legal purveyor of almanacs to Englishmen—produced almanacs in three types: sheet, pocket, and book.

Printed in decorative red and black, sheet almanacs such as *Wing's Sheet Almanack*, the *London Sheet Almanack*, or the *Cambridge Sheet Almanack* functioned like wall calendars do today. Consumers pinned sheet almanacs to their walls to display a calendar grid for the entire year, usually accompanied by a table of lunar phases, sunrises, and prominent constellations. In addition, the Company sold two pocket almanacs, *Rider's* and *Goldsmith's*. These also consisted of a single rubricated (red-and-black) sheet, but instead of pinning the whole sheet flat, pocket almanacs were cut to miniature size and stitched together for portability.

Book almanacs were composed of no fewer than two full sheets cut and stitched into booklets. The Company developed two kinds of book almanacs: blanks and sorts. Differences between them lay in the amount of paper used (blanks typically consisted of two and a half sheets, sorts had only two), rubrication (blanks had their first and second sheets printed in black and red, sorts had only the first), and their calendar format (blanks used a full opening for each month, but sorts showed only one month per page). The Warehouse-Keeper sold book almanacs unbound, but retailers often interleaved book almanacs with blank sheets for note taking and diary keeping and sold them in bindings of varying quality.

Both blanks and sorts contained a variety of information. Almost all contained weather predictions; dates for the terms (Michaelmas, Lady's Day, etc.); a regal table listing English monarchs and the dates of their reigns; instructions for astrological farming, tide tables, and a historical chronology; detailed information on comets and eclipses; and rising and setting times for the sun, moon, and major constellations. Depending on the title, a customer might also get lists of fairs and major highways (sometimes with a woodcut map), formats for drawing up legal documents, tables for calculating interest, tables of weights and measures, or instructions for basic surveying. Many almanacs included essays on astronomy, astrology, and mathematics—along with some bad poetry. Because most almanac makers had been astrologers since the sixteenth century, sorts were often divided into two sections: a calendar and an attached "ephemeris" or "prognostication." Occasionally the ephemeris included its own title page, which (if separated from the calendar) could lead one to consider it a separate work altogether. Some nonastrological sorts retained this two-section format, substituting informational essays or tables for prophecy in the ephemeris section. Blanks usually integrated their astrology into their roomier two-page calendars, but a few included an ephemeris with seasonal prophecies to supplement their monthly predictions.[2]

The Rhythm of Production

Appropriately for a calendar, production of the Stationers' Company almanacs followed a consistent annual rhythm. The sale of the almanacs—like the Ash Wednesday feast, the Election Feast, and the Lord Mayor's Day parade—composed part of the Company's immutable annual regimen. Since the early eighteenth century, the Company Clerk had placed an advertisement announcing the impending sale of almanacs in an early October edition of the *London Gazette*. Occasionally a separate advertisement appeared in early November proclaiming the sale date for "blanks and sorts almanacks."[3] This amounted to a ritual affirmation of the Company's changeless sale dates: sheet almanacs would once again be sold on the third Tuesday in October, and book almanacs would be sold on the third Tuesday in November. This Tuesday tradition lasted until well past 1850.[4]

The process of preparing for these fall Tuesdays began in May when the Master and Wardens contracted for the year's supply of almanac paper.[5] Like most customers of print shops, the Company provided the paper for its projects to its printers. It should be noted at this point that although this study does not address papermaking, the English Stock monopoly might have given the Company significant influence on the overall price of paper during the eighteenth century. The Stock must have been the largest single customer for English papermakers, and one assumes that its volume of consumption gave it some influence among paper producers. At the same time, early modern paper was entirely handmade, so it was quite scarce relative to demand. A paper mill at maximum production in 1739 yielded no more than eight reams per day. The physical limits of production—and the consequent scarcity of the commodity—may have been sufficient to outweigh any leverage that would normally accrue to a bulk consumer. Whatever sway the Company may have enjoyed, paper still constituted the single largest cost in almanac production. Cyprian Blagden estimates that paper consumed something on the order of 43 percent of almanac production capital, as compared to 33 percent for composing and printing and 24 percent for compiling. This is high compared to the 20.5 percent that Colin Clair calculates for normal book production, but even the lower figure is staggering compared to modern costs. Whether the Company succeeded in lowering the cost of paper or not, a cursory look indicates that paper was as precious to the Company as it was to a private consumer. Regulations for the Warehouse-Keeper described (in some detail) his responsibilities for recycling wastepaper and tracking paper stocks.[6]

Compilers' copies came due in July. When the famed sixteenth century astrologer William Lilly came down with his fatal illness, Henry Coley traveled to his home at "the beginning of every summer" to compile Lilly's almanac by dictation, not leaving until he had "despatched them for the press," presumably in midsummer or late summer.[7] Francis Moore completed the copy for his first edition of *Vox Stellarum* by 6 July 1700, and he was evidently complying with a venerable deadline.[8]

A 1716 contract with George Parker required him to submit his copy by 24 July.[9] Logic dictates that the fruit of their labors went to press in August—certainly no later than mid-September. Surviving receipts for printing work tend to confirm this. Mary Harrison received payment in August or September from 1767 to 1772 for printing almanac sheets.[10] During the 1770s, some other printers took payment later in the year (one as late as February 1779) but this was usually because they printed multiple impressions to compensate for unanticipated demand for individual titles. Regardless, initial impressions had to be in the warehouse for sale on the big Tuesdays in October and November.

So many merchants purchased almanacs that the Warehouse-Keeper found it expedient to have blank contracts printed up prior to sale dates.[11] These contracts assumed that retailers would buy more than they could pay for, and then would repay the Stock in three installments due in mid-December, early May, and late September of the following year. The long debt cycle indicates that both the Company and retailers saw almanac sales as a low-risk investment. Demand for them was so consistently strong that profits were all but guaranteed. Timing thus became exceedingly important in this lucrative but highly seasonal trade. Having almanacs on the shelf even a couple of days before the competition could translate into big money, and the Stock-Keeper probably padded his salary by selling early to a few favored retailers. By 1780 the Court had attempted to crack down on this practice, stating explicitly in its "Rules Orders and Instructions for the . . . Treasurer or Warehouse keeper of the Stock of this Company" that the Warehouse-Keeper had no right to "Sell or deliver out any Almanacks until the time of the general Sale to be appointed by the Master Wardens and Stock-keepers of the Company for the time being or the Major part of them." Evidently this had been common practice beforehand, and one suspects that as the assistants' vigilance waned, it became common practice afterward too.[12]

English retailers sold their almanacs, whether legal or illegal, in December. The overwhelming majority of convictions for "selling an Almanack liable to a Stamp Duty, ye same not being stamped or markd" occurred in late December, and the patrons of such unlucky entrepreneurs were undoubtedly holiday shoppers.[13] Like calendars today, almanacs made natural Christmas and New Year's gifts. Folklorists list books among traditional English New Year's gifts; being cheap, individualized, and intimately connected with the calendar, book almanacs would have filled that bill nicely. The Stationers' Company, of course, always chose almanacs for its holiday gifts.[14] The Bishop of London traditionally received complimentary, handsomely bound copies of Stationers' Company almanacs on 23 December, and the Archbishop of Canterbury also received a set around the same time. Bernard Capp believes that these ceremonies symbolized the Company's submission to ecclesiastical censorship, and while this may have been true in an earlier era, there is little evidence to indicate that these gifts were more than ceremonial traditions by the turn of the eighteenth century. One nineteenth century folklorist claims that the Archbishop of Canterbury's gifts were a symbol of gratitude for his generosity to the crew of the Stationers' barge during the Lord Mayor's Day celebrations.[15] The Company used almanacs at other times in the same way that companies today use pencils and baseball caps with corporate logos; the Warehouse-Keeper was officially obligated to provide "Almanacks to the Master and Wardens for Presents or New Years gifts as hath been accustomed." By the nineteenth century the Company was not alone. *Notes and Queries* mentions a hatter who gave round sheet almanacs imprinted with his business address—suitable for storage in a hat crown—as gifts to his holiday customers.[16]

Sales and Profits

This production process generated huge profits throughout the eighteenth century. The sheer numbers of almanacs involved had significant implications for early modern Britain.

The market for book almanacs declined by about a third from the seventeenth to the eighteenth centuries, but even this reduced volume was still staggering. In the late seventeenth century, the Company produced an average of about 323,000 book almanacs per year and sold about 95 percent of that annual stock. In the late eighteenth century, they produced approximately 238,000 almanacs every year, and although no good sales figures exist for later eras, there is no reason to believe that the Company lost its ability to read demand. The 95 percent sales figure offers a reasonable marker regardless of chronology.[17] If production decreased somewhat, annual profits of around £1,000 to £1,500 in the late seventeenth century nearly doubled to about £2,000 in the late eighteenth century.

Even where records of production and profit are scarce, indirect evidence confirms that the almanac trade was extremely lucrative. Since the mid-sixteenth century, the Company had found it economical to buy out competitors. The English Stock paid large annual sums—usually £200 per year but straying up to £500 by the end of the seventeenth century—in order to secure exclusive production rights from universities and individuals who occasionally received competing patents. One inevitably concludes with Capp that "the large sums involved [in these buy-outs] reflect the continuing profitability of the trade."[18] If almanac sales in and around 1711 did happen to run counter to these trends, there is no mention of it in Company records. The English Stock had yielded a "full dividend" of 12.5 percent since 1703, indicating that its almanac mainstay continued to put in a strong performance.[19] The wholesale value of the Company's almanac inventory stood at £2,767 in 1709, £2,763 in 1710, £3,694 in 1711, and £4,150 in 1712. Such values compared favorably with the previous historic high of £3,418 in 1682.[20] All of this inductive evidence indicates that in 1711, as in decades before and hence, several hundred thousand book almanacs entered the English marketplace legally during the five weeks between the Tuesday sale and New Year's Day. This represents a remarkable feat of logistics in a time when goods moved at horse-cart speed and credit moved at the speed of paper.

If production figures for almanacs in 1711 are imprecise, the nature of their consumption remains almost entirely elusive. Supply has always been much easier to document than demand, and even though we can be certain that English consumers bought hundreds of thousands of almanacs every year, this fact offers little insight into the significance of that consumption. How many English subjects actually read the almanacs they bought, and how they might have interpreted what they read, must remain largely the province of speculation.

Capp believes that during the seventeenth century yeomen, husbandmen and artisans bought the vast majority of almanacs, but Paul Wiggins suggests a level of "widespread popularity" during the eighteenth century that could not have been class-specific.[21] A predominantly rural market would tend to explain why book almanac production did not increase in proportion to the population during the eighteenth century. An increasingly urbanized demographic meant that personal access to information became more widespread. The incentive to pay for a compendium of information such as the almanac, which could provide everything from intellectual stimulation to entertainment, may not have been the same in a city as in the countryside. Likewise, urbanization would not have diminished the need to mark the passage of time, and this helps to explain why production of sheet almanacs—essentially wall calendars—quadrupled even as book almanac production decreased by a third.[22]

Yet, the heyday of sheet almanacs did not last beyond the 1770's, and by 1787, the relative prominence of sheet and book almanacs had permanently reversed. Wiggins attributes this to a narrowed "cost differential" between book and sheet almanacs resulting from "competition and increases in stamp duty" without a commensurate improvement in the content of sheet almanacs.[23] This purely economic explanation does not invalidate urbanization as an indicator of almanac readership, but it does qualify it significantly.

Despite this relative decline in market share, a bit of simple math indicates that the Company printed some 25 million book almanacs over the course of the eighteenth century, and almost all of them sold within a month of publication. This figure cannot begin to include the hidden tide of illicit almanacs that accompanied the Company's annual production, but even the legal volume taxes the imagination. The volume, consistency, and duration of its consumption made the book almanac into the juggernaut of early modern English popular literature. It merits study as a perennial force "both shaping and reflecting the beliefs and practices of the period."[24] Surely it is reasonable to suggest that English people commonly "saw their own lives as a seamless whole, their calendar of birth, love, ambition and death imprinted on the almanac of great events."[25]

Notes

1. The Stamp Act of 1711 (Statute 9 Anne Cap: 23, Section 23) sets the rates for an "Almanack or Kalendar for any one particular year." Worshipful Company of Stationers, "Series 1—Box B: 'Almanac, Primer and Bible Printing: Infringement of Patents,'" in *Records of the Worshipful Company of Stationers 1554–1920*, ed. Robin Myers (Cambridge: Chadwyck-Healey, 1985), 98: Folder A1. See also the Stationers' Chancery complaint cited in R. P. Bond, "John Partridge and the Company of Stationers," *Studies in Bibliography: Papers of the Bibliographical Society of the University of Virginia*, Vol. 16 (Charlottesville: Bibliographical Society of the University of Virginia, 1963), 65. For the point phrased in broader terms, see Bernard Capp, *English Almanacs 1500–1800* (Ithaca, NY: Cornell University Press, 1979), 284. Additionally, consider the Court of Assistants' criteria for pressing charges against possible interlopers in the later section on piracy. The question of whether or not a sham almanac violated the Company's patent always depended on whether or not it contained a calendar.

2. Cyprian Blagden, "The Distribution of Almanacks in the Second Half of the Seventeenth Century," *Studies in Bibliography: Papers of the Bibliographical Society of the University of Virginia*, Vol. 11 (Charlottesville: Bibliographical Society of the University of Virginia, 1958), 110; Capp, *English Almanacs*, 30, 33, 41, 245.

3. "Almanacks of all sorts for the Year 1711 will speedily be published at Stationer's-Hall, London, viz. Rider, Goldsmith and Sheets on the 24th In-

stant, and Blanks and Sorts on the 21st of November next." J. Tonson, "The London Gazette, 5 October to 7 October 1710," in *Early English Newspapers*, ed. Susan M. Cox and Janice L. Budeit (Woodbridge, CT: Research Publications, 1983). "On Tuesday the 23d of October next will be Publish'd at Stationers-Hall these following Almanacks, Stamp'd according to the Direction in the late Act of Parliament. London Sheet and Cambridge Sheet, at 6s. each per Quire; Raven Sheet at 6 s. per Quire. Riders Almanack unbound at 40s. per Hundred; and Goldsmith's Almanack unbound at 32 s. per Hundred. The Sheet Almanacks, Rider and Goldsmith's Almanacks, will be published. Notice shall be given of the time of Publication of Blanks and Sorts Almanacks." Benjamin Tooke and John Barber, "The London Gazette, 4 October to 6 October 1711," in *Early English Newspapers*, ed. Susan M. Cox and Janice L. Budeit (Woodbridge, CT: Research Publications, 1983). "At Stationer's Hall on the 21st of October, and the Blanks and Sorts on the 25th of November." Benjamin Tooke and John Barber, "The London Gazette, 11 October to 14 October 1712," in *Early English Newspapers*, ed. Cox and Budeit (Ibid.).

4. The last advertisement for the Tuesday sale in the Company's archives is dated 1835. It indicates that by this time the sale of both sheet and bound almanacs had been consolidated to the third Tuesday in November. An 1873 advertisement marks the earliest evidence of a non-Tuesday sale. Worshipful Company of Stationers, "Series 1—Box C: 'Almanac Accounts and Advertisements,'" in *Records of the Worshipful Company of Stationers 1554–1920*, ed. Robin Myers (Cambridge: Chadwyck-Healey, 1985) 98.

5. The Wardens spent two shillings "with the Master and Capt Phillipps when wee went about paper for Almanacks" on 13 May 1705. Worshipful Company of Stationers, "Wardens' Accounts 1663–1728," in *Records of the Worshipful Company of Stationers 1554–1920*, ed. Robin Myers (Cambridge: Chadwyck-Healey, 1985) 76.

6. Blagden, "Distribution of Almanacks," 113; Colin Clair, *A History of Printing in Britain* (New York: Oxford University Press, 1966), 207–8. A 1780 list of regulations for the Warehouse-Keeper states that he could only purchase and distribute paper with the written consent of the Master, Wardens, and a majority of the Stock-Keepers, "Rules Orders and Instructions for the . . . Treasurer or Warehouse keeper of the Stock of this Company." Stationers, "Series 1—Box M: English Stock and Irish Plantation (Manor of Pellipar) 1673–1964," Folder 6. For late eighteenth century paper production considered in terms of labor and industrial history, see Leonard N. Rosenband, "Productivity and Labor Discipline in The Motgolfier Paper Mill, 1780–1805," *Journal of Economic History,* 45, 2 (1985), 435–43; Idem., "The Competitive Cosmopolitanism of an Old Regime Craft," *French Historical Studies* 23, 3 (2000), 455–76.

7. Edward Heron-Allen, "Coley, Henry," in *The Dictionary of National Biography from the Earliest Times to 1900*, ed. Sir Leslie Stephen and Sir Sidney Lee (Oxford: Oxford University Press, 1921–22), 784–85. See also Bernard Capp, "Coley, Henry," oxforddnb.com.

8. Gordon Goodwin, "Moore, Francis," in *The Dictionary of National Biography from the Earliest Times to 1900*, ed. Sir Leslie Stephen and Sir Sidney Lee (Oxford: Oxford University Press, 1921–22), 796.

9. "Articles of Agreement . . . between George Parker of Salisbury Court London Student or Practicioner in Astrology . . . and Joseph Collyer Warehousekeeper of the Company of Stacioners London for and on the behalfe . . ." Stationers, "Series 2—Box 33: Legal Papers (1680–1893), 112."

10. Stationers, "Series 1—Box M: English Stock and Irish Plantation (Manor of Pellipar) 1673–1964," 104, Folder 6.

11. See an example dated 1750 in Ibid., Folder 4.

12. Ibid., Folder 6. See also a the broadside advertisements for every year from 1738 to 1772 preserved in the Company's archives. All list the sale date for book almanacs as the third Tuesday in November. Stationers, "Series 1—Box C: 'Almanac Accounts and Advertisements,'" 98.

13. The Company's archives contain a considerable number of notices of conviction for selling pirated almanacs between 1758 and 1775. A few are dated in February, and one in March, but these exceptions prove the rule: almanac sales were highly seasonal. Stationers. "Series 1—Box B: 'Almanac, Primer and Bible Printing: Infringement of Patents,'" 98, Folder 5.

14. A. R. Wright, *Fixed Festivals, January–May, Inclusive*, vol. 2 of *British Calendar Customs—England*, ed. T. E. Lones (London: William Glaisher, 1938), 24.

15. Most years, the Wardens spent money on the Bishop's almanac ceremony. See, for example, entries for 23 December 1702, 1703, 1704. Stationers, "Wardens' Accounts 1663–1728," 76.

16. Stationers, "Series 1—Box M: English Stock and Irish Plantation (Manor of Pellipar) 1673–1964," 104, Folder 6.

17. These figures are drawn either directly or by interpolation from Blagden, "Distribution of Almanacks," 114; Cyprian Blagden, "Thomas Carnan and the Almanack Monopoly," *Studies in Bibliography: Papers of the Bibliographical Society of the University of Virginia*, Vol. 14 (Charlottesville: Bibliographical Society of the University of Virginina, 1960), 40.

18. Blagden, *Stationers' Company: A History*, 194–97, 203; E. Leaton Blenkinsopp, "Christmas Almanacs," *Notes and Queries: A Medium of Inter-Communication for Literary Men, Artists, Antiquaries, Genealogists, Etc.*, 7 February 1880; Capp, *English Almanacs*, 37–38, 240.

19. Mismanagement in the 1670s and 1680s had led to austerity measures for the English Stock in the 1690s. Beginning in 1694, dividends were sharply curtailed for the first time in decades. The early eighteenth century saw the tail end of this episode, with 9 percent dividends ordered on 1 December 1701 and 18 December 1702. Subsequent dividends were a "full" or "whole" 12.5 percent, as

evidenced by entries for 20 December 1703, 4 December 1704, 3 December 1705, 7 December 1706, 1 December 1707, 6 December 1708, 5 December 1709, 4 December 1710, and 19 December 1712. The dividend entry for December 1711 is missing altogether, probably because of a clerical oversight. Stationers, "Court Book G; Fair Copy of Court Minutes 8 November 1697 to 6 May 1717," 57.

20. Blagden, "Distribution of Almanacks," 109.

21. Wiggins, 55. But see his entire second chapter for a nuanced (and necessarily inconclusive) discussion.

22. Ibid., 114; Blagden, "Thomas Carnan and the Almanack Monopoly," 40.

23. Wiggins, 44, 53.

24. Capp, *English Almanacs*, 292.

25. Simon Schama, *Citizens: A Chronicle of the French Revolution* (New York: Vintage Books, 1989), xvi.

᧭ Chapter Four ᧮

Almanac Piracy

*A*s in every other genre of early modern print, legal almanacs had
to compete with illicit almanacs. Ironically, individual stationers
led the way in piracy, but this illegal trade was not a free-for-all. Stationers' Company leadership enforced a tacit code of conduct among
Company pirates, which allowed the Company to preserve both its profitable monopoly and its social cohesion. In 1711, the Royal government
inadvertently assumed responsibility for enforcing the almanac monopoly, which reduced some of the internal tension inherent in the Company's dual role as pirate safe house and pirate victim. This dynamic requires the reexamination of some scholarly assertions about early
modern literary piracy and the Company's response to it.

The Rules of the Game

Historians writing about almanacs invariably mention piracy.[1] Lucrative profits generated dozens of knockoffs "Printed and Dispersed in
several Parts of England" that encroached continually on the Company's
turf. Because English consumers appear to have cared more about price
than patents, catching poachers required both constant vigilance and a
continual propaganda effort designed to establish that "all Almanacks
which are not Printed for and Publish'd by the Company of Stationers, at
their Warehouse in Stationers-Hall, are Counterfeit . . . Sham Predictions
and Prognostications."[2] Enforcement became all the more complicated because the pirates were, as often as not, also members of the Company. A
brief look at early eighteenth century piracy prosecutions indicates that
piracy was an accepted practice governed by an unwritten code of ethics.

The decade prior to 1711 saw its share of shady dealing. Indeed,
it started right off with a rather audacious insider scam job, which was

run out of the Company's warehouse itself. Benjamin Tooke, a livery-man and well-respected bookseller, had been serving as the English Stock's Warehouse-Keeper for fifteen years when the assistants caught him cooking the books in 1702. As the Stock printers delivered their finished work—notably almanacs—Tooke paid them in full with Stock money. He then recorded a smaller amount of work received, and sold the surplus for his own profit. At a general meeting of the English Stock in July 1702, the shareholders agreed that they "had bin greatly injured," and Tooke was sacked and sued accordingly.[3]

Looking at the situation from a modern perspective, one assumes that a scandal of this magnitude must have shaken the Company from top to bottom. Reprisals must have been swift and unrelenting; heads must have rolled; people must have talked. At the very least, one assumes that old man Tooke—whose betrayal stood out all the more because of the respect he had previously enjoyed—must have been ostracized so-cially, stripped of his professional privileges, and skewered to the full ex-tent of the law. But none of this happened. To be sure, the Court tight-ened procedures immediately, establishing a

> Standing Rule for the future that no one Printer doe Deliver his part of an Impression of any work or printing that hee shall doe of the Companys till the other printers have printed off and are ready to deliver their respective parts yt so the whole Impression of such Bookes may bee Delivered and brought in Compleate together and Delivered into and kept in the Stockkeepers Warehouse. And further yt whatever monys or Charge shall bee Entered in the Cheque Book and for which the Treasurer is accountable a Not of such monys or Charge bee taken out by the warden for the Time being immediately after every Court and delivered by him to the Stockkeepers att their next meeting successively. And yt such monys and Charge to be Entered to the Stockkeepers Account.

But though the Company garnished his dividend in lieu of payment, Tooke retained his livery share in the Stock; by allowing him to keep his share, the Stationers' Company was essentially subsidizing his penalty. The Company filed three suits in Chancery against him, but pursued them at a leisurely pace—and dropped them entirely in favor of arbitration by 1704. The process remained amicable; the Warden's accounts for Sep-tember and October 1704 indicate that arbitration and payment proba-bly occurred over drinks. Tooke's son certainly experienced no fallout for his father's indiscretions. On the contrary, Ben Jr. became Jonathan Swift's preferred bookseller, rapidly acquired a hefty fortune, received a patent as the Queen's printer, and served as printer to the City of London. In 1705, with this case still fresh on the Company's collective mind, John Dunton wrote his autobiography with at least the partial intent of ingratiating himself with the Company leadership. Instead of villainizing Ben Sr., Dunton chose to call him "the Ingenious Took, that was formerly Treasurer." Ben Jr., Dunton asserted, was likewise "truly Honest, a man of refin'd Sense (or cou'd never have been related to Ben Took) and is unblemish'd in his Reputation." Far from swift and relentless, the Company's justice was leisurely and ambivalent, almost benevolent. The example they made of their treacherous Warehouse-Keeper looked, for all the world, like an open invitation to other would-be pirates.[4]

Other piracy cases of the era followed the same pattern. On 17 April 1701, the Court determined to proceed against John Bradford (a yeoman since 1681) for publishing "a Sham-Sheet Almanack and also a little Book called Ephemeris." Bradford came from the class of stationer most likely to produce pirates. Lowly yeomen with no stake in the Stock could hardly be expected to refrain from "invading . . . the Companys right of printing and publishing . . . all manner of Almanacks" without the threat of severe consequences. If profits were paramount, the Company had every incentive to crush Bradford—yet he was still a member in good standing four years later when he freed his apprentice, Richard Griffin, at a monthly Court meeting.[5]

As the Benjamin Tooke case demonstrated, however, even the greatest among the stationers were not immune from the temptations of almanac profits. On 4 May 1702, the Court learned that Thomas Hodgkins—an assistant sitting in that very meeting—had printed for John Taylor (yet another member of the Company) "a Booke intitled an *Ephemerides of the Coelestiall motions for Six years* . . . wherein there is a Calendar which is the Coppy right of the Company." To compound the situation, the offending *Ephemerides* was "Calentated by John Wing"— one of the Company's own most venerable almanac compilers. If Tom Hodgkins—assistant, shareholder, and contractor of the English Stock— was not above piracy, then everyone was a suspect. It seems the Court took this for granted, and the Master gently "Ordered yt Mr Hodgkins doe not deliver nor Mr John Taylor sell any more of the said books till further satisfaction be made to ye Compy therein." Gentlemen did not prosecute gentlemen, even if gentlemen did cheat the English Stock. In the end, Hodgkins kept his Company contracts, his Stock shares, and his position on the Court; Wing continued compiling sorts and blanks; and the Court chose John Taylor to be Assistant Renter Warden in March of the following year.[6]

There were certain exceptions to this general leniency. The first decade of the eighteenth century saw three particularly entertaining piracy cases—one involving a nonstationer, and two featuring members and employees of the Company. The first—a struggle with the prominent Tory astrologer George Parker—lasted for over a decade. The second—a tiff with one of the Company's most notorious almanac makers, John Partridge—lasted for four years. This latter case overlapped with a third to make Partridge simultaneously a pirate of the Company and the victim of another stationer pirate. These three cases delineate the limits of the Company's evident ambivalence toward its own profit margins.

It should be noted at the outset that George Parker was no ordinary almanac maker. He enjoyed the patronage of two highly placed scientists—astronomer Edmund Halley and the Great One Himself, Sir Isaac Newton.[7] Partridge's actions should be seen in light of the considerable latitude these connections must have afforded him. Whether or not he was legally insulated or simply a stubborn old cuss, his antics absorbed much of the Court of Assistants' time during the first decade of the eighteenth century, and his case reveals much about literary piracy during that era. On 2 June 1701, the Master reported to the Court of Assistants

> That he and the Wardens had attended Mr Cooper Councellr att Law and advised with him abt printing & publishing of . . . a Little Booke called *a double Ephemeris* printed and published by George Parker and sold by him and Mr Grunt a Bookbinder whether the printing & publishing of them was within the Companys Right and Patent and that the said Mr Cooper was clearly of opinion it was, whereupon Itt was ordered that the persons concerned in the printing and publishing the said sheet and Book be proceeded against at law or in Chancery.

The printer of Parker's *Double Ephemeris* was David Edwards, a yeoman stationer. Edwards had only gained his freedom in 1691, but this was already his second run-in with publishing law. In 1698, he had violated the English Stock patent by printing "30 or 40 gross of Black and White Primers" for a bookseller named William Spiller. Despite his status as an inveterate poacher, once he agreed "not to Print or Publish or cause to be printed or Published any more of the Compys Almanacks or Kalendars or any other of the Companys Coppys," the Court decided to "not proceed any further against Mr Edwards." Parker fared less well.

By the end of July, the old Tory submitted himself to the judgment of the Court of Assistants. He agreed to pay £50 toward the Company's legal fees and to give bond against violating its patent again, and the Court graciously dropped its case in Chancery.[8]

Parker, however, could not restrain himself. Early in 1704, the Court summoned Samuel Bridge (a stationer since 1683) "to show Cause why hee printed the Ephemeris wherein is the Company's Calendar without their leave." He freely admitted to buying the copyright to the book from Parker and to printing 2,000 copies of it. The Company Clerk was implicated in this because he had allowed Bridge to secure legal ownership of the copyright by having it entered in the Stationers' register. The Court's response mirrored its previous actions almost exactly. It dropped all disputes with its own member after Bridge agreed to post a bond and refrain from further poaching, and Parker again took a bigger hit than his stationer accomplice. After some initial recalcitrance in March when he "insisted [that] The Booke . . . was not a Calendar," he finally "owned his fault." As it had in 1701, the Court agreed to let Parker post bond for good behavior and to "accept of a summe of money as he was able to pay and not to bee proceeded against him at Law hee being poor."[9]

In August 1709, the Court ordered "that Mr Parkers almanack be received by the Company for this Year upon reasonable Termes." Parker responded with what he considered to be reasonable terms: the publication of two titles, not one, for a fee proportional to sales rather than the usual flat fee.[10] Shortly thereafter the negotiations misfired, and by early December the Court was again dragging Parker into Chancery. It considered "whether there is not a Kallender in his Ephemeris"; the Master "produced the Bond from Geo Parker to the Company"; and the Court agreed "that he should be sued on his said Bond." This time the Court failed even to mention a printer, but this may well have been because Parker had acquired his own press in the interim. A subsequent contract between him and the Company stipulated payment not only for compiling almanacs, but also for printing them. Printers were not legally obligated to join the stationers' guild, so the Company would have had no means of preventing him from setting up shop. For a polemicist (and determined almanac pirate) such as Parker, owning a press guaranteed him access to the market and a platform for his ideas. It also enabled him to subvert the Company's monopoly without relying on collaborators among its own members. How he managed to establish a press, "hee being poor," is a mystery until one considers his patrons.[11]

This feud continued intermittently until 1716. In that year, as usual, Parker printed 1,700 copies of his *Ephemeris* without the Company's "Order Consent or Allowance." This time, however, the old printer/almanac maker reached a workable arrangement with his nemesis. The Company persuaded him to sell the unauthorized almanacs he had already printed through the warehouse at Stationers' Hall and to "deliver the Manuscript copy" of all future almanacs to the warehouse for the rest of his life. In return for this small concession, the stationers promised him three full rubricated sheets for his almanac, as compared to the normal maximum of two rubricated sheets normally allowed for blanks. Since he was also a printer, the contract guaranteed him English Stock patronage: the Company would hire him to print his own works. As a guarantee that Parker would not play both pirate and employee, the Company would hire a different firm to print one sheet from each of Parker's works. However, in lieu of that one sheet he was guaranteed a contract for two sheets from other almanacs—both to be printed in numbers commensurate with his own. Parker's persistent piracy persuaded the Court to expend a considerable amount of its patronage in order to buy him out. The remarkable thing is that he came to terms at all. However, in the aftermath of the Hanoverian succession and the 1715 uprising, Parker's reputation as a High Tory Jacobite no doubt rendered his public position somewhat less secure. Although he probably retained the patronage of some powerful men, association with the impeccably loyal Stationers' Company was a politically wise move on Parker's part. Conversely, the arrangement allowed the Company to demonstrate its value to the Crown by bringing a notorious pro-Stuart agitator under control.[12]

At about the same time as the Court was making its 1709 overtures to Parker, one of its longtime employees—John Partridge—decided to demand a higher fee for compiling his *Merlinus Liberatus*. Perhaps because Isaac Bickerstaff had conclusively demonstrated Partridge's death the year before, the Court turned him down. Bickerstaff's goading must have put Partridge in a fighting mood; instead of capitulating to his erstwhile employer, he sold his copy to printer John Darby Jr., who proceeded to print several thousand copies. Darby was a second-generation stationer; he had gained his freedom by patrimony in 1697 and took over his father's shop at Bartholomew Close in 1704. Never prone to haste, the Court negotiated throughout July 1709, attempting to resolve "Some matters in Difference between the Company and Dr. Partridge Conserning his Almanack for the Year Ensueing." Neither side budged, and the

Company moved from negotiation to active coercion. In a move clearly directed at Darby, it ordered

> That the Master and Wardens and whom else they shall think fitt do goe into such printing houses as they have reason to suspect are printing any of the Companys Coppys or Almanacks to see whether they are printing any of the Companys Coppy's.

It also opened negotiations with Partridge's longtime antagonist, George Parker, and sought and received an injunction from the Lord High Chancellor prohibiting Partridge and Darby from marketing *Merlinus Liberatus*. In early October, the Company publicly advertised this injunction on handbills and in newspapers.[13]

Partridge and Darby responded by seeking the high ground politically. They complied with the injunction by keeping their copies of *Merlinus Liberatus* off the market, but they contested it in Chancery. They then took their case to the public. Seeking to identify their cause with the ruling Whigs, Darby printed "A Letter to a Member of Parliament" in which Partridge argued quite forcefully that the Company's patent rested on the principle of sovereign royal prerogative that had been replaced by "Revolution-Principles" in 1688. As he portrayed it, Partridge was not trying merely to sell an almanac; he was "contending for the just and undoubted Rights of Parliament, and the Fundamental Constitution of the Legislature." The Company, of course, had its own spin. Its Chancery complaint warned that if the monopoly were not supported, "poor Widows & Orphans must perish." Hyperbole notwithstanding, the injunction held, and Partridge and Darby ate the cost of producing the 1710 edition of *Merlinus Liberatus*.[14]

The entire incident harmed none of the participants, and probably helped most. The Company, of course, kept its monopoly, and even reinforced it by securing legal sanction for it under yet another monarch. Partridge did not publish an almanac again for two years, but his stubbornness paid off handsomely in 1713 when the Company rehired him at the unheard-of rate of £100 per year. And Darby did well for himself in spite of his losses on *Merlinus Liberatus*. He was wealthy enough to contribute three guineas—more even than some assistants—to an emergency fund for a fellow printer in 1713.[15]

Ironically, Partridge's conscientious compliance with Chancery injunctions could not prevent other pirates from publishing on his behalf. As word got around that *Merlinus Liberatus* would be suppressed,

Benjamin Harris—stationer and notorious literary troublemaker—took it upon himself to liberate the title. Harris had been selling books since acquiring his freedom in 1670. An inveterate gadfly, the government prosecuted him twice for pro-Protestant agitation during the 1680s. He quit London for Boston where he published America's first newspaper, *Publick Occurrences*, in 1690. Puritan authorities promptly banned it. Back in London by 1695, Harris started looking for an edge in the almanac market. He began spicing up his copies of Partridge's *Merlinus Liberatus* in 1702 by adding a few pages of his own, and continued doing so until the Company obtained an injunction against him in 1708. It must have come as no surprise when "a false Almanack of Partridges . . . wherein is a Kallender and Suspected to be printed and published by Benjamin Harris" appeared on 4 December 1709 at the height of the Parker and Partridge disputes. The Master soon "Acquainted the Court that it would be very Necessary to have some Advertisement Concerning Benja Harris publishing Partridges Almanack with the Companyes Kallender," and the Stationers' Company added another bill in Chancery to their long list of lawsuits for 1709.

This hardly slowed the man down. In fact, Harris added Parker to his list of counterfeits in 1710, changed his Partridge to "Patridge" (note the dropped "r"), and began pasting sections of authorized sheet almanacs into ersatz book almanacs with the notion of rendering them technically legal. The Company Clerk naturally refused to enter "the Almanack or Coppy of Benjamin Harris a Member of this Company called Merlinus Liberatus" into the official copy register, and the Company spent the next five years publicly denouncing Harris and prosecuting him annually in the same court for the same infraction. Harris thus earned the dubious distinction of being the only stationer of the early eighteenth century to be aggressively pursued and publicly ostracized by the Court.[16]

Harris could be the exception that proves the rule. The Court did not pursue him because of his inferior rank in the guild, nor from a sense of special outrage over his betrayal. Of the ten almanac pirates named in this narrative fully two-thirds were insiders, and only Harris endured any significant penalty as a result of his piracy. Old Benjamin Tooke and Thomas Hodgkins ensured that the pirate ranks included stationers of position and prestige,[17] but the Court offered its no-fault forgiveness to most common pirates too. Yeomen such as John Bradford, John Taylor, David Edwards, and Sam Bridge suffered no greater penalty than their livery and assistant counterparts. None of them except John Darby endured anything even remotely like the persecution of Harris, and Darby's difficulty had an extremely confined impact on his career.[18]

A similar pattern emerges from a look at the three nonstationer pirates. Two of them, Wing and Partridge, were Company retainers at the time of their offenses. Of these two, Wing kept his job while Partridge temporarily lost his. Both Partridge and Parker endured sustained legal assaults by the Court—and as a result, their pocketbooks suffered in ways that Wing's did not.

This difference in the Court's treatment of nonstationer pirates mirrors the distinction between Harris and other stationer pirates. In all instances, it took considerable efforts to raise the Court of Assistants' ire. Not even Tooke's inside job could spark the sort of ruthless war that the assistants waged in Chancery against Harris, Parker, Partridge, and Darby. These four posed a threat to something far more significant to the Company than a few pounds and pence. Where the others infringed on English Stock profits, these men jeopardized the almanac monopoly itself. In general, all stationers enjoyed a sort of tacit right to almanac piracy—but only so long as they observed certain rules. Rule number one was: once caught, do not resist. Ritual repentance—public acknowledgement of the Court's authority and the Stock's monopoly rights—was all that the Court required. After that, everything else was negotiable—even extensive monetary damage such as that inflicted by Benjamin Tooke.

This rule of obeisance, more than anything else, explains why the Court pursued Harris with such special intensity. He was the sole stationer to persistently—even creatively—defy the Court's authority; in doing so, he threatened more than profits. Partridge and Darby questioned the almanac monopoly and held their ground, but they did so on principled grounds and implicitly acknowledged that they might be wrong by obeying the Chancery injuction. Their disagreement with the Court was respectful, formal, and limited, and as such left room for distinction between the monopoly and the Court of Assistants' authority as a body. Harris, on the other hand, refused to recognize the Court's authority in any way. His aggressive, indiscriminate profit seeking ignored both the English Stock monopoly and the Company's right to regulate his behavior. By disrupting consensus and deference, he undermined the social fabric of his guild. The Court's legitimacy was as much at stake in the Harris case as the Stock's legal title to the almanac trade. Profit margins may have been negotiable—consistently high demand gave the Court considerable room for leniency after all—but authority was a less flexible commodity.

This conclusion tends to modify an assertion made by Adrian Johns in his influential work, *The Nature of the Book*. He states that

> The Stationers' court's procedures were those of a commercial and civil conversation, the primary imperative being to pacify antagonists by consent rather than to distinguish a felon and execute a punishment. Only when the Company itself was plaintiff did this cease to be the case. The moral and commercial order of printing and printed books was consequently constructed in terms appropriate to this domain, and not, say, in the language of natural rights to which eighteenth-century polemics would later resort.[19]

Evidence from the early eighteenth century confirms the flexible, civil nature of the Company's legal methods, but Johns overestimates the Company's aggressiveness as a plaintiff. He alleges that the Company never budged when its own bottom line was at stake. Perhaps this was true in the seventeenth century, but during the early eighteenth century the stationers did not see their interests in purely monetary terms. Rather, they consistently weighed communal politics in the same balance as English Stock income. Although the Company was, by definition, always the plaintiff in cases of almanac piracy, it only pressed its case as a last resort. Extreme situations such as Partridge and Darby's opposition to its monopoly forced the Company into an aggressive stance, but the most notable characteristic of its legal actions against almanac poachers was their leniency. The Company's preference for "commercial and civil conversation" over legal finality did not end where Company interests began.

Implications of the Stamp Act of 1711

Just as the Wardens were placing orders for the paper that would become the almanacs of 1712, a sea change occurred in the world of almanac piracy. Parliament passed a Stamp Act which, while raising revenue for the central government, had the side effect of strengthening the English Stock against piracy.

Only rarely does a committee divine its own best interests, and the Stationers' Court was no exception. In spite of its potential benefits, the Court fought the Stamp Act of 1711 tooth and nail. The Master, bookseller William Phillips, called an emergency meeting on 14 May 1711 to

"Consider what is most proper to doe to prevent the said Duties being laid . . . on Almanacks." The assistants also hedged their bets, preparing for the worst by rechecking the precise number of almanacs sold during the previous season. Early June saw a momentary burst of optimism as the Company's lobbying efforts during the previous weeks appeared to have paid off. The assistants ordered

> That the thanks of this Court be given to the Master Wardens and Mr Beckley their Clerke for the Care they have taken and the good Service they have done for the Company relating to the Bill now depending in the House of Comons for laying a duty upon all Almanacks.

Hope quickly gave way to disappointment, however, as the bill passed in mid-June and the Court settled down to "consider of the manner and number of Almanacks to be printed this yeare by reason that they must be stamped."[20]

The act could not have passed at a worse time in the rhythm of almanac production. If it had passed the previous autumn, the Company would have had time to raise its prices. They could then have funded the extra expense in 1711 with profits from 1710. By passing the act in June 1711, however, Parliament imposed on the Company a sudden spike in production costs without allowing time for it to accrue enough capital to compensate. As if this were not enough, the act established a three-month deadline for payment of the stamp tax. If they had followed their normal rhythm of production by buying stamped paper in early August, the tax payment would have come due before the third Tuesday in November. Only the profits from October's big Tuesday sale of sheet and pocket calendars would have been available at that point, which might not have been enough.

To minimize capital outlay, the Court decided to cut real production costs. It ordered "that all the Red letters shall be left out with printing of all Almanacks both Sheet and Sticht for the future and only upon Black Letters," and that "there be not above halfe the Quantityes [of almanacs] printed off at first and that there be care taken that they be printed upon good paper and with a good letter." It also attempted to persuade the Lord Treasurer to allow them to print their almanacs before having them stamped. This would have delayed the three-month payment deadline and placed it after both big Tuesday sales, allowing the Company to fund the stamp tax out of its own profits. Maddeningly, the Lord Treasurer waited until mid-August to turn them down, and the Court reluctantly shifted its attention to finding

> Such persons as [the Master] shall think fitt that will undertake duly to answer the moneys for Stamping of Paper for Almanacks from time to time as occasion shall be they having the benefitt of prompt paymt.

Master Phillips was not so easily thwarted, however. He side-stepped the Lord Treasurer and "with some difficulty prevailed with the Comisioners of the Stamp Office to take a Bond under the Comon Seale of this Company for paying the duties on Stamping of Almanacks" dated from mid-September. This placed the payment date well after the third Tuesday in November, allowing the Stock to fund its debt with the profits from that year's sales. The Company's almanac credit crisis became manageable even as English Stock printers were inking type for the first impression.

As the initial panic calmed, the Court began formulating ways to economize other than by simply reducing the production cost and shuffling bond dates. In early August, the Company reconsidered its blanket decision to print all almanacs in black ink only. Sheet almanacs, after all, became part of a purchaser's decor—or they might have been all the decor a purchaser could afford. Either way, color was integral to its purpose, so a sheet almanac without red ink might have lost more customers than usual to illegal competition. Accordingly, the Court backtracked a bit and decided to print sheet almanacs "in Red and Black Letters as they have been for severall yeares," but at the additional cost of "a penny . . . to the full price besides the Stamps." English households would not have to choose between beauty and legality after all.[21]

Having cleared these initial hurdles, the Court would soon find that the Stamp Act had strengthened its commercial position immensely. Parliament had attached part of its financial fortunes to the Company's almanac monopoly. Henceforth, selling a pirated almanac would impinge not only on the stationers' profits, but also on Her Majesty's revenues. The Court no longer had to police its own; the Crown's revenue officers would do that job.[22] Individuals selling unauthorized almanacs were convicted—and convicted quickly—not for violating the Company's patent but for "selling an Almanack liable to a Stamp Duty, ye same not being stamped or markd as directed by the Statute."[23] The Company's advertisements in London papers would soon offer rewards to people informing not on pirates who violated the royal patent of 1603, but on those who violated the Parliament's Stamp Act of 1711.[24]

Instead of Company lawyers, pirates now faced the resources, vigilance, and coercive authority of a sovereign government guarding its revenue. Legal actions by the Company could now be limited to the high-profile pirates such as George Parker who possessed enough political influence to persuade the Stamp Commissioners to provide them with legal paper. Despite its vigorous lobbying against the bill, the Company soon came to consider the Stamp Act of 1711 to be a bulwark of its prerogative, and the Stationers' Company spent its own time and treasure working for its enforcement. As the nature of this development became clear, it probably influenced renegades such as Partridge and Darby to come to terms.

In the late eighteenth century, after the Court of Common Pleas and the House of Commons finally struck down the almanac patent, the Stamp Act actually saved the English Stock's dominance. Although finally free to operate in the open, would-be competitors still had to buy stamped paper. The Company lobbied actively for ever-higher stamp taxes until, by the turn of the century, it was the only publisher which could afford to capitalize almanac production. The Company adapted well to a changing relationship between political authority and economic power, trading royal monopoly for capitalist monopoly.[25]

Almanacs and Literary Piracy

Almanac piracy has significant implications for our understanding of early modern literary piracy in general. Johns claims that the concept of piracy cannot be limited to legal definitions:

> [A strictly legal definition] tends to assume static definitions of entities—in both the book trade and the law—that in fact were fluid throughout the [early modern] period, literary property being an evident example. Moreover, any such approach will still radically underestimate the extent of piracy as experienced by contemporaries . . . Ultimately, no legalistic definition will be satisfactory because the improprieties referred to by contemporaries were not simply legal ones. They permeated the domains of print, occupying the far more amorphous territory of civility.[26]

Almanacs were, if anything, more subject to piracy than any other category of printed matter in early modern England. For sheer quantity of pirated works and perennial persistence, few could match the almanac pirate. Yet it is difficult to imagine a reasonable definition of almanac piracy that extended beyond the law.

This is because almanac piracy was not a question of literary property or precise information, but of market access. When George Parker agreed to allow the Warehouse-keeper to sell his pirate almanacs, they became legal. Nothing about the books themselves changed, only their point of sale. Almanac pirates were not pirates because they copied the unique contents of the Company almanacs; pirated almanacs were, as often as not, simply supernumerary copies produced on the sly by the English Stock printers themselves. Almanac pirates were pirates because they transgressed the Company's exclusive right to market that particular genre of literature. The question was not what a pirated almanac contained but who sold it. If in other categories of printed matter the line between piracy and plagiarism, or between production and authorship became blurred, the almanac case indicates that in other genres, the question was not complex at all. Almanac piracy in early eighteenth-century England had nothing to do with substance, and everything to do with form—legal form.

In light of such an understanding, some of Johns' more careless generalizations about early modern readership must also be modified. Johns claims that piracy subverted trust so that readers constantly questioned the authenticity of printed materials:

> If piracy was as widespread as commonly feared [during the early modern period], then trusting any printed report without knowledge of those processes could be rash. Profound problems of credit thus attended printed materials of all kinds. Without solutions there could be few meaningful uses for books—and perhaps no durable reasoning from them . . . Print, and piracy in particular, consequently gave rise to fierce concern for the verification of any and all printed materials.[27]

Almanacs, of course, were printed materials, but it strikes one as a bit absurd to imagine "fierce concern" over their derivation. Insofar as they identified themselves with their work, compilers may have worried about piracy, but they collaborated with pirates too often to make a serious case for such concern. The Stationers' Company only worried about particular sorts of piracy—that which threatened its social authority or its legal monopoly—and this had nothing to do with the trustworthiness of almanac content. Similarly, the government worried about every sort of piracy after 1711, but its concern was for reliable revenue, not reliable knowledge.

Almanac consumers (we do not know enough about their habits to call them readers) seem to have shared the producers' lack of concern about piracy. The Stamp Act made the identification of pirated almanacs easy: a prospective consumer could identify pirated wares by checking for an official stamp. Consequently, if almanac consumers' primary concern was "verification of any and all printed materials" one would expect a precipitous decline in the illicit almanac trade after 1711. Yet, stamp or no stamp, almanac piracy continued undiminished. The sheer numbers of pirates both inside and outside Company ranks indicates a strong and enduring incentive for pirates. This implies not "fierce anxiety" but high demand.

Even so, consumer enthusiasm for pirated almanacs does not mean that Johns' assertion is entirely off the mark. We are, after all, discussing entirely different genres of print. Although amateur scientists produced them, almanacs were simply not intended for the type of "durable reasoning" pursued in academe. A profound functional gap separates durable conceptual works such as Newton's *Opticks* and transient utilitarian literature such as Moore's *Vox Stellarum* (not to mention newspapers, advertisements, ballads, etc.). They required entirely different levels of precision to serve their respective purposes. So it seems reasonable to imagine that "profound problems of credit existed" only for particular kinds of printed matter.

Notes

1. Blagden, "Distribution of Almanacks," 113–14; Blagden, *Stationers' Company: A History*, 173, 188, 216, 234–35; Capp, *English Almanacs*, 38–40, 45–47, 268–69.

2. Quotes from an advertisement placed by Company Clerk Nathanael Cole on 11 October 1737. Stationers, "Series 1—Box C: 'Almanac Accounts and Advertisements,'" 98.

3. Blagden, *Stationers' Company: A History*, 205; D. F. McKenzie, ed., *Stationers' Company Apprentices 1641–1700*, vol. 2 (Oxford: Oxford Bibliographical Society, 1974), 144, 167; D. F. McKenzie, ed., *Stationers' Company Apprentices 1701–1800*, vol. 3 (Oxford: Oxford Bibliographical Society, 1978), 352, 413; Nichols, *Literary Anecdotes*, 606; Henry R. Plomer, *A Dictionary of the Printers and Booksellers Who Were at Work in England, Scotland and Ireland from 1668 to 1725* (Oxford: Bibliographical Society, 1922), 293; Stationers, "Court Book G; Fair Copy of Court Minutes 8 November 1697 to 6 May 1717," 57.

4. Blagden, *Stationers' Company: A History*, 205; Dunton, *Life and Errors*, 288; Nichols, *Literary Anecdotes*, 73; Stationers, "Court Book G; Fair Copy of

Court Minutes 8 November 1697 to 6 May 1717," 57, Stationers, "Series 1—Box M: English Stock and Irish Plantation (Manor of Pellipar) 1673–1964," 104, Folder 6; Stationers, "Wardens' Accounts 1663–1728," 76.

5. McKenzie, ed., *Stationers' Company Apprentices 1641–1700*, 19, 25; McKenzie, ed., *Stationers' Company Apprentices 1701–1800*, 46; Stationers, "Court Book G; Fair Copy of Court Minutes 8 November 1697 to 6 May 1717," 57.

6. Stationers, "Court Book G; Fair Copy of Court Minutes 8 November 1697 to 6 May 1717," 57.

7. Johns, *Nature of the Book*, 543–46.

8. McKenzie, ed., *Stationers' Company Apprentices 1641–1700*, 18, 51; McKenzie, ed., *Stationers' Company Apprentices 1701–1800*, 114; Plomer, *Printers and Booksellers*, 111; Stationers, "Court Book G; Fair Copy of Court Minutes 8 November 1697 to 6 May 1717," 57.

9. McKenzie, ed., *Stationers' Company Apprentices 1641–1700*, 20, 160; Stationers, "Court Book G; Fair Copy of Court Minutes 8 November 1697 to 6 May 1717," 57.

10. See the letter of George Parker to the Court of Assistants 2 August 1709 in Stationers, "Series 2—Box 33: Legal Papers (1680–1893)," 112.

11. Stationers, "Court Book G; Fair Copy of Court Minutes 8 November 1697 to 6 May 1717," 57.

12. See the "Articles of Agreement . . . between George Parker of Salisbury Court London Student or Practicioner in Astrology . . . and Joseph Collyer Warehousekeeper of the Company of Stacioners London for and on the behalfe . . ." in Stationers, "Series 2—Box 33: Legal Papers (1680–1893)," 112.

13. R. P. Bond, 63–67; McKenzie, ed. *Stationers' Company Apprentices 1641–1700*, 44–45; McKenzie, ed., *Stationers' Company Apprentices 1701–1800*, 99; Plomer, *Printers and Booksellers*, 97–98; Stationers, "Court Book G; Fair Copy of Court Minutes 8 November 1697 to 6 May 1717," 57.

14. R. P. Bond, 64; Stationers, "Series 1—Box B: "Almanac, Primer and Bible Printing: Infringement of Patents," 98, Folder 4.

15. R. P. Bond, 78–79; Nichols, *Literary Anecdotes*, 62.

16. R. P. Bond, 70–75; McKenzie, ed., *Stationers' Company Apprentices 1641–1700*, 159; McKenzie, ed., *Stationers' Company Apprentices 1701–1800*, 20, 73; Plomer, *Printers and Booksellers*, 145–46; Stationers, "Court Book G; Fair Copy of Court Minutes 8 November 1697 to 6 May 1717," 57.

17. The seventeenth century was no different. As Johns notes, "Pirates were therefore not a distinguishable social group. They existed at all ranks of the Stationers' community, and at times were among its most prominent and upstanding members." Johns, *Nature of the Book*, 167.

18. Blagden's observation on the Tooke affair could be extended to include most instances of stationer piracy: "The gentle treatment of erring Stock

servants is one of the more pleasant aspects of the casualness with which Stock and corporation affairs were conducted during the reigns of the later Stuarts." Blagden, *Stationers' Company: A History*, 205.

19. Johns, *Nature of the Book*, 221.

20. Stationers, "Court Book G; Fair Copy of Court Minutes 8 November 1697 to 6 May 1717," 57.

21. Ibid.

22. 10 Geo. II. fol. 546 put extra teeth into the government's enforcement effort: "If any Person shall hawk, carry about, utter, or expose to Sale, any Newspaper, &c. not stamped according to Law, it shall be lawful for any Justice of the Peace, upon Conviction of the Offender, either by his own Confession, or by the Oath of One or more Witness or Witnesses, to commit such Offender to the House of Correction for any Time not exceeding Three Months: And any person may seize and carry any such Offender before a Justice of the Peace, who, upon producing a Certificate of such Conviction, under the Hand of the Justice of the Peace, is intitled to a Reward of Twenty Shillings, to be paid by the Receiver-General of the Stamp Duties." Stationers, "Series 1—Box C: 'Almanac Accounts and Advertisements,'" 98.

23. Stationers, "Series 1—Box B: 'Almanac, Primer and Bible Printing: Infringement of Patents,'" 98, Folder 5.

24. "Whereas an Act passed in the 10th Year of the Reign of Queen Anne, 1712. laying several Duties on Paper, &c. P. 299. This Clause is inserted, All Books serving to the Purpose of an Almanack, by whatsoever name entituled, shall be charged with those Duties, by the Act made in the first Session of this Parliament. This Notice is therefore given, to prevent Persons incurring the Penalty of the said Act, which is Ten Pounds upon all such as shall sell any Almanack, not stamped, or any thing serving the Purpose of an Almanack, according to the Direction of the Said Act." Tooke and Barber, "The London Gazette, 11 October to 14 October 1712."

25. Blagden, "Thomas Carnan and the Almanack Monopoly," 35–36.

26. Johns, 162.

27. Ibid., 30,173.

❧ Chapter Five ❧

Almanac Authorship

*A*lmanac makers were, at best, only partially responsible for almanac content. Because almanacs were commodities produced by a corporation for mass consumption, their contents reflected the priorities of the market and of the Stationers' Company itself, not those of an individual compiler. This notion complicates recent assertions about early modern authorship.

Remuneration: Compiler as Commodity

Almanac authors worked for money, although many claimed it was not enough. During their ill-fated negotiations in 1709, George Parker advised the Court of Assistants "to encourage their Authors better than they have formerly done. For when their pay will not answer the time spent about such business that a person is retain'd to do, that undertaking must of necessity be slightly perform'd."[1] Few can argue for a raise as artfully as a professional writer.

Special pleading notwithstanding, compilers' fees varied widely depending (primarily) on public prominence. Big names drew big salaries while anonymous compilers had to content themselves with a pittance. During the seventeenth century, Capp observes that compilers of "sorts" received 40s. per edition. At the opposite extreme, astrologer William Lilly earned £70 per year. Lilly's less popular colleague Henry Andrews began by earning £2, and progressively increased his fee to £15 by the end of his life.[2]

This fame-based pattern continued through the eighteenth century. In 1709, Parker claimed that £5 was evidently the standard fee—"no more than what they pay others, and what they paid me for my first Copy."[3] Again one wonders how much Parker distorted the picture to his own advantage. John Partridge (as we have seen) ended his days with £100 per year, and Parker received lucrative guaranteed printing contracts in addition to a share in his almanacs' annual profits. The Court of Assistants awarded Mr. Raven £20 for his sheet almanac in August 1704, and on 10 September 1705 voted £20 to "the psons Employed in procureing . . . the Small London Plate Almanack."[4] The rather well-known compiler Tycho Wing earned £17 for compiling several titles in 1743.[5] In mid-century Robert Heath, erstwhile compiler of two popular sorts titles (*The Ladies' Diary* and *The Gentleman's Diary*), reported that the Company paid ten guineas for the former and three guineas for the latter.[6] John Baker stated that "the sum of three Guineas is the least I can take for the time and trouble" of correcting a sheet almanac botched by another compiler in 1770.[7] Thomas Wright received a mere £6 6s. for compiling *Seasons Almanack for the Year 1775*,[8] while in 1786 and 1787, Charles Hutton—"Doctor of Law [and] Professor of Mathematicks in the Royal Academy"—signed contracts to compile six book, two sheet, and two pocket almanacs for the handsome sum of £130 guineas per year—more than double Parker's standard £5 per title. In 1788, Henry Andrews of Royston in the county of Hartford signed a similar contract, but being neither a doctor nor a member of the Royal Academy he earned a mere £20 for compiling all of the Company's almanacs.[9] Andrews had been compiling at least one almanac—*Old Moore's*—since 1778, and he continued with this title until 1820. Despite the consistent success of that title, he evidently never earned more than £25 a year.[10]

The pattern of remuneration during both the seventeenth and eighteenth centuries is clear; aside from a few notable exceptions such as Lilly, Partridge, and Hutton, most almanac compilers earned small fees ranging from £3 to £20, and the almanac makers of 1711 were doubtless no exceptions. Prestige, productivity, and name recognition determined the relative value of a compiler to the Company. Normally the Company took its time in distributing paychecks to compilers. Most fee receipts and other references to payment indicate that compilers got their money sometime between March and June of the year following publication. If compilers typically submitted their copy in July, this represented a twelve-month delay. All in all, wise almanac makers did not quit their day jobs.

Cash, however, was not the only form of remuneration. Capp suggests that almanac makers also worked for the prestige of publicity and the political and legal legitimacy that a contract with the Stationers' Company conferred on an astrologer.[11] More tangibly, almanac compilers were normally allowed to include advertisements for their businesses in the almanacs they wrote.[12] The records place no explicit cash value on this subsidy, but one could speculate that it equated to a 10s. bonus, plus the value of any custom that such nationwide advertisements might have attracted.[13]

They may have griped occasionally about the Company's parsimony, but compilers still kept knocking on the warehouse door. Since it was the only legitimate employer for an almanac maker, the Company never had to recruit compilers unless it sought someone with the eminence of a Royal Fellow. The lesser fellows came to them. Well-known astrologer and longtime almanac maker John Gadbury initiated negotiations for printing his *Ephemerides* with the Company in September 1703.[14] In August 1704, Mr. Raven proposed a sheet almanac and had it approved. Some seven decades later, Henry Hughes begged for his deceased father's spot as a compiler, "having done Wing's Almanack only two Years, and single sheets of three others only one."[15] Whatever its fees, people sought the Company's almanac patronage. For its part, the Company treated almanac makers as commodities. It paid them for services rendered, but it felt no compunction to preserve their work as a reflection of their individual creativity. The primary function of the almanac was to make profits for the English Stock, not to provide a showcase for authors.

Dead Authors, Brand Names

In the finest Grub Street tradition, eighteenth century almanacs were almost entirely the products of anonymous hacks, and this is a singularly important fact if one wishes to interpret almanac content intelligently. During the eighteenth century especially, the name on an almanac title page functioned increasingly as a brand name; it was not intended to identify the contents with a particular person. This lack of attribution marks the almanac as a literary commodity and offers early evidence for the "consumer revolution" which characterized eighteenth century popular culture. It also complicates Johns's model of authorship and readership and shifts interpretive focus from the biases of individual compilers to the Stationers' Company's motives as a corporate author.

Three of the nineteen almanacs used in this study listed no author at all on their title page. These included *Fly*, *Swallow*, and *Poor Robin*. *Fly* and *Swallow* traced their lineage back to Cambridge University. From the 1620s to the 1640s, the Cambridge University Press created a series of fictional almanac authors named for birds and water features. "Jonathan Dove" led off in 1627, and was followed shortly thereafter by a flock of others, including Mr. Fly and Mr. Swallow.[16] At Cambridge and then at London, *Swallow* was published continuously for over a century from 1641 until 1746.[17] *Fly* lasted for nearly as long—from 1657 to 1752.[18] *Poor Robin*, of course, was written by Poor Robin. William Winstanley (a notorious Royalist biographer from Saffron Walden, Essex) invented this wisecracking persona in 1664, but whereas Winstanley died in 1698, Robin lived on at Stationers' Hall until 1776—and bootleg compilers resurrected him occasionally for several years thereafter.[19]

Robin's ghost was not alone. Dead men wrote eight of the eighteen almanacs in the 1712 sample. Henry Coley, protégé of the famous seventeenth century astrologer William Lilly, founded the *Merlinus Anglicanus Junior* series in 1686. He died in 1707, but the stationers continued to publish *Merlinus Anglicanus* until 1755—always with Henry Coley's name on the title page.[20] We have no evidence that Nathaniel Culpepper, the ostensible compiler of *Culpepper Revived*, ever even existed. Nicholas Culpepper (a popular astrologer-physician) died in 1654, and Nate may well have been one of Nick's "numerous offspring." Whether the Stationers' Company invented him or not, however, *Culpepper Revived* continued to list Nathaniel Culpepper as its author from 1680 until 1751—a bit longer than most people, even an astrologer, could have been expected to live.[21]

Like Nate Culpepper, George Rose left no historical evidence of his existence except that the Stationers' Company published an almanac in his name for sixty-one years from 1656 until 1717.[22] Thomas Fowles first published *Speculum Uranicum* in 1680, and after his death at Ticehurst Parish in 1703 someone else did him the favor of compiling subsequent editions until 1712.[23] Francis Perkins, a "well-willer to mathematics," started compiling the Perkins series in 1655. Nothing else is known about him except that his series remained in publication for almost a century.[24] Thomas Trigge died five years after the first edition of *Calendarium Astrologicum* hit the market in 1660, but the series continued in his name until at least 1746.[25] Thomas White was a surveyor and dial maker living in Toddington, Bedfordshire. In 1677, he took over compilation of a successful almanac series created by William White—a grocer, amateur astronomer, nonconformist, local Toddington celebrity and very likely Thomas's father. There is no evidence to indicate whether Thomas was still alive in 1711, but it is certain that the Company continued publishing *White* until at least 1778, by which point the original namesake would have been over one hundred years old.[26] John Woodhouse first published his almanac in 1610. By 1711, he had been dead for several decades, but he was still the author of *Woodhouse*.[27] Nor was this practice of posthumous naming a new trend. As early as 1660, John Tanner was complaining that

> [almanacs] from dead carcasses are raised like flies . . .
> Whose fathers thrice ten years were dead and rotten
> Before their feigned offspring were begotten.[28]

By the early eighteenth century, it was common knowledge that the stationers employed "all ye dead Authors" to write their almanacs.[29]

The few compilers lucky enough to actually be alive in 1712 eventually added their names to the stable of dead authors. The titles compiled by Richard Saunders, John Tanner, and Richard Gibson either expired with or pre-deceased their founders. The other four compilers—William Andrews, John Tipper, Francis Moore, and John Wing—created titles that outlived them by decades. The most notable thing about Richard Saunders is that there was two of him. The original Richard Saunders was an astrologer-physician and an "old and valued friend" of legendary almanac makers William Lilley and Henry Coley. He first published *Apollo Anglicanus* in 1656, but a second compiler named Richard Saunders—probably the first Richard's son—took over the series in 1683. This second Richard Saunders—a surveyor, dialer, and mathematician working out of Leicestershire—was decidedly not an astrologer. He continued to compile his antiprophetic *Apollo Anglicanus* until 1737.[30] John Tanner first published *Angelus Britannicus* in 1657, a year after Saunders entered the market. He died in 1715, and—like the second Saunders—his death marked the end of his series.[31]

Richard Gibson's *Astrologus Britannicus* enjoyed nothing like the longevity of these old titles. It lasted a mere six years from 1707 to 1712. The Hampshire schoolmaster continued publishing other items until 1724, so lack of popularity rather than death terminated his career as almanac maker. No doubt his *Astrologus Britannicus* failed to sell in adequate numbers, and the Company finally cut its losses. As Capp notes, "unsuccessful authors were ruthlessly axed" by the Company.[32]

Unlike the ill-starred Gibson, William Andrews had been compiling almanacs for over fifty years by 1711. He practiced astrological medicine, and like the original Richard Saunders he had enjoyed the sponsorship of William Lilly. Andrews entered ghostwriter status in 1713, and his name and his *Great News from the Stars* survived until 1764.[33]

John Wing's name appeared on the title page of *Olympia Domata*. If the trade ever saw anything like a dynasty, it was the Wing family of Rutland—which produced three generations of famous almanac compilers. Vincent Wing, a surveyor and astrologer from North Luffenham,

published the first edition of *Wing* in 1643 and continued compiling it
sporadically over the next twenty-five years until his death in 1668. The
eminent astronomer John Flamsteed considered Vincent's almanacs to
be "the exactest" of the era. His nephew John, a surveyor-astrologer
from Pickworth, took over the title's compilation in 1680 and combined
it with *Olympia Domata* that same year. After John's death in 1726, his
nephew, Tycho Wing, continued compiling the family titles. By 1730,
Tycho was also compiling *Merlinus Anglicanus, Great News from the
Stars,* and *Vox Stellarum* for the stationers, and his portrait still hangs in
Stationers' Hall: an author among bookmen. *Olympia Domata* remained
in print until at least 1805.[34]

John Tipper single-handedly invented a new kind of almanac. Mas-
ter of Bablake School in Coventry, he founded the highly respected
Ladies' Diary in 1704, which was intended to offer intellectual diver-
sion to middle-class women—but also to provide a venue for publishing
the work of Britain's leading mathematicians. The rapid success of *The
Ladies Diary* led the company to grant him another title, *Great Britain's
Diary: or, The Union-Almanack,* in 1710. After Tipper died in 1713,
Great Britain's Diary lasted only until 1728, by which date the Act of
Union had become old news. *The Ladies' Diary,* however, exhibited extraordinary staying power; its editors included fellows of the Royal Society such as Henry Beighton, Thomas Simpson, and Charles Hutton,
and it remained in constant publication until 1840. A genteel hybrid
called *The Ladies' and Gentlemen's Diary* lasted for another three
decades until 1871.[35]

Only Francis Moore's almanac, *Vox Stellarum,* was destined to out-
last the titles founded by Tipper and Wing. Moore was an astrological
physician, sometime assistant to John Partridge—and like Partridge, a
vociferous Whig. Advertisements indicate that he sold "an excellent
Worm-Powder [and gave] judgment on Urine, or the Astrological way,
which is surest, without seeing the Patient . . . [at a residence] near the
Old Barge House in Christchurch, Southwark." He was forty-three years
old when he compiled the first edition of *Vox Stellarum* for 1701. He
continued to compile that title until his death in 1714 or 1715. In 1712,
nobody could have predicted *Vox Stellarum*'s legendary success, but
by midcentury the title was selling more copies than all other book
almanacs combined. It lasted over two hundred years, entering the
twentieth century as *Old Moore's Almanac.*[36]

Advertisements in some of the ghostwritten almanacs indicate the
identity of their actual compilers. *Perkins* carried two ads for "William
Baynham, Student in Astrology and Physick, at the Blue-Ball, the Corner

of St. Andrew's-Street, the Upper-End of St. Martin's-Lane, near the Seven-Dials, St. Giles." Although no further information can be found on Baynham, his occupation fits the classic profile for an almanac maker, and it seems likely that he was one of the compilers content to receive the Company's £2 fee. The only ads in Trigge's *Calendarium Astrologicum* were for Francis Moore's medical practice, which indicated that he authored the 1712 edition. John Wing apparently compiled two titles in addition to *Olympia Domata*. These were *Fly*, and *Culpepper Revived*, and *Fly*'s only advertisement was for a book called

> *Astronomologia, vel Urania Practica, Rediviva*: being the Astronomical Treatis, formerly published by Vincent Wing, and William Leybourn, Revived. Very much amplified and augmented, by the Surviving Author, and John Wing Nephew the Deceased.

Similarly, *Culpepper Revived* carried an ad for John Wing's surveying services. Coley's *Merlinus Anglicanus* advertised Joseph Pepper, a mathematician and tutor "at Stamford in Lincolnshire." Capp lists Pepper as one of John Wing's associates in a circle of East Midlands compilers that grew up around the Wing dynasty—making Pepper a likely compiler.

Identities of the anonymous compilers for *Poor Robin, Swallow, Speculum Uranicum, White,* and *Woodhouse* remain uncertain, but this lack of information only serves to highlight the larger pattern of almanac authorship. Thomas Trigge died in 1665, but *Calendarium Astrologicum* lasted until 1746. Nicholas Culpepper died in 1654, but *Culpepper Revived* lasted until 1737. Henry Coley died in 1707, but *Merlinus Anglicanus* lasted until 1730. William Andrews died in 1713, but *Great News from the Stars* lasted until 1764. Nobody knows when Francis Perkins died, but his almanac lasted for ninety-one years from 1655 to 1746. *Woodhouse* lasted over a century from 1610 to at least 1712, and it was still prominent enough at the end of its run to be worth pirating. Tycho Wing died in 1750, but *Olympia Domata* endured into the nineteenth century. Tipper died in 1713, but the *Great Britain's Diary* outlived him by fifteen years, and *The Ladies Diary* was still running strong in the 1830s. And of course, Francis Moore's *Vox Stellarum* became a fixture in British popular culture and outlasted all the rest. As the eighteenth century progressed this became increasingly common until, by the 1770s, every almanac maker was pseudonymous.

The conclusion is unavoidable: for early modern almanacs, the author's name functioned as a brand name, not a source attribution.

Each of "ye dead Authors'" names indicated a particular style and mix of content. English consumers thought of Henry Coley and William Andrews like today's consumers think of Eddie Bauer and John Deere—or perhaps more appropriately, Robert Ludlum and Stephen King. This becomes all the more apparent when one considers the long-term success of almanacs listing no author at all. *Poor Robin* lasted for a century and a half. *Fly* ran for ninety-five years from 1657 to 1752, and *Swallow* endured even longer from 1641 to 1746. Richard Saunders, the deceased human being, competed for shillings side-by-side with Poor Robin, the fictional character; consumers gravitated to a given brand name because it signified content, not authorship. The almanac genre, then, straddled the line between literature and commodity. It was the quintessence of *Dunciad* culture, the embodiment of everything that Alexander Pope despised about early modern print.

The Dead Authors in America

The trademark function of author names was transatlantic. A teenaged Benjamin Franklin spent over a year and a half in London in 1724–26 working for English printers.[37] Seven years after his return, he founded the most famous early American periodical—and probably the best-known almanac in history. His *Poor Richard* was clearly a close cousin to the English *Poor Robin*. Franklin probably intended the similarity to hint at his ironic tone, while the difference—a more formal name with the pedigree of kings behind it—may have indicated the earnest worldview embodied in his aphorisms about work, money, and marriage (a marked departure from Robin's whimsical flippancy). More telling than his title, however, was Franklin's choice of pseudonym: none other than the venerable "Richard Saunders, Philom."[38] Franklin would have had small motive to use the Company's old compiler if American consumers were not already familiar with the brand, so his decision contributes another scrap of evidence for cultural interchange across the British Atlantic, as well as for the strong "mimetic impulse" toward Britain in colonial American culture.[39]

Yet Franklin did not intend his pseudonym as a tribute to the motherland. His decision to place Richard Saunders instead of Benjamin Franklin on his almanac covers exemplified early modern marketing savvy. Consumers not familiar with Franklin's name would have instantly recognized Saunders, and they would have known that the choice of names was anything but random. Richard Saunders was the earliest anti-astrological compiler in the Company's pantheon; he published *Apollo*

Anglicanus free of prognostication since 1684. If in the idiom of eighteenth century British popular culture "Poor Robin" meant "outrageously satirical almanac," then "Richard Saunders" meant "venerable antiastrological almanac." Both symbols, like Franklin himself, were entirely unfriendly to prophecy. Since Saunders was still alive in 1733 (he would not die until late 1736 or early 1737), Franklin may have implied a personal tribute as well. Without a doubt, however, his title and brand-name pseudonym symbolically announced both his position on astrology and the style and tone of his almanac's content.

By using these symbols, Franklin gained a marketing advantage over his competitors. The ironic mixing of idiomatic conventions— jocular Poor Robin with sober Richard Saunders, both antiprophetic— would itself have piqued consumer interest. Almanac readers having to choose between Franklin's product and another local almanac would have been enticed to investigate how successfully *Poor Richard* mimicked the styles associated with Stationers' Company products. Small wonder that even as his personal fame increased, Franklin kept the pseudonym and the title intact. Additionally, by retaining Saunders's name for two decades after the old compiler's death in 1737, Franklin mimicked the Company's commercial decision to print dead authors. The death of the real Richard Saunders had no effect on the constellation of meanings attached to his name; he, like all the other dead authors, lived on as a byword in commercial idiom. Saunders alone, however, received his posthumous voice from an American colonist. One wonders whether the old Leicestershire philomath would have approved.[40]

It is perhaps going too far to claim that the author's name signaled merely a trademark and not a person. This is an unnecessary dichotomy. It would be more appropriate to say, ". . . and not a *real* person." As far as readers were concerned, the text before them *was* the author. Experience strongly suggests that when Franklin's readers read his almanac, they did not—*could* not—think of it as a voice from nowhere. They personified the text. They had an image of the speaker in mind, and after Franklin himself gained fame that image may have included Franklin's own face. Readers may have even thought that they knew Franklin himself, or at least knew what he would be like if they met him. From the tone and message of the text, they could have imagined what his tastes were, whether he would have been a helpful friend, an annoying neighbor, or a hopeless conversationalist. But whether or not these images had any relation to the actual Franklin whatsoever is irrelevant. Images of authors—that is to say, of the voice in a text—grow out of interpretation; they cannot be a prerequisite for it. Nevertheless, they are a common byproduct of reading. In this sense, texts are authors. Poor Robin could have been as real an author as John Tanner, and to the extent that a generic almanac such as *Swallow* had an imaginable persona, it too was an author. The dead authors had an active life of their own so long as they had an active, living reader.

Almanacs and the Consumer Revolution

As commodities, almanacs offer early evidence of the eighteenth century "consumer revolution" described by J. H. Plumb, John Brewer, and Neil McKendrick.[41] The massive annual volume of almanac sales indicates that the lineaments of a consumer society (in the form of a functional system of production and distribution) existed already in the early eighteenth century, as well as an avid market with money to spare for luxuries. Use of almanacs as Christmas and New Year's gifts indicates some early commercialization of these holidays. Similarly, that the Stationers' Company paid a small group of specialists to produce a wide variety of titles suggests a consumer-driven process—an implicit recognition that in spite of the Company's monopoly, its almanacs still had to cater to a variety of individual preferences in order to turn a profit. The use of packaging to present each almanac as a unique product despite numerous commonalities in their content only reinforces this notion. If McKendrick suggests that the consumer revolution can only be seen in full swing during the latter half of the eighteenth century, almanacs point to early roots indeed.[42] And this is precisely what one would expect if, as Plumb asserts, the advent of cheap printing was the catalyst and prerequisite for the entire phenomenon.[43] At the same time, the pervasive trend toward old titles and old names in the almanac trade indicates that novelty was not an essential characteristic of the consumer revolution.[44] The almanac commodity, at least, depended on nostalgia rather than fashion for its market appeal.

Almanacs and Early Modern Readership

Recognizing almanacs as commodities and almanac readers as consumers tends to complicate recent thinking about early modern authorship. Adrian Johns disputes Elizabeth Eisenstein's thesis that the unprecedented dissemination of standardized texts in early modern Europe injected "fixity" into intellectual discourse.[45] He demonstrates that early modern printing was an artisinal process rather than the mechanical one envisioned by Eisenstein. Interpretive liberties taken by compositors, publishers, proofreaders and censors combined with transcription errors and piracy to alter the original meanings of a manuscript. The "author" of a printed text was actually the publishing community rather than a single writer. To this point, Johns' argument supports the notion of corporate authorship presented in this paper. Yet he draws some unwarranted conclusions from this observation. Since "authorship itself was a collective enterprise . . . [and] attribution to any one individual was retrospective, contingent, and contestable," Johns believes that "For seventeenth-century <u>readers</u>, as for modern historians, apportioning creativity was rarely straightforward."[46] Because the Company controlled book production,

> Isolating a consistent, identifiable, and immutable element attributable to the individual author would be virtually impossible. . . Attributing authorship was thus intensely problematic for both contemporary and future <u>readers</u>. *A priori*, virtually any element in a work might or might not be the Stationers' responsibility, in virtually any field of writing.[47]

As a result of this, there was

> One concern in particular that possessed early modern <u>readers</u> . . . Could a printed book be trusted to be what it claimed? . . . A central element in the <u>reading</u> of a printed work was likely to be a critical appraisal of its identity and its credit . . . <u>Readers</u> worried about who decided what got into print, and about who controlled it once it was there.[48]

The theme in all this is trust. In Johns' thinking "authorship and authority" are equivalent terms. Readers wanted to trust books. They gave their trust when they thought that a trustworthy person wrote their books. The vital link in the construction of knowledge lay between the author and the reader.

This is a curious argument. Perhaps the most notable thing about authorial authority is that so many early modern writers made no attempt to claim it. Johns focuses on writers who wished to be viewed as trusted authorities and genuinely wanted their exact words to reach an audience intact. Such authors clearly existed, but one might legitimately wonder if they represent a majority case, or if they were exceptional. After all, early modern England was chock full of printed matter published under assumed names. Pen names were the order of the day, particularly in non-scholarly writing. The nameless Grub Street scribbler dashing off copy for his supper was a staple caricature of early modern culture. Political pamphlets, fiction, ballads, and almanacs all regularly appeared without attribution; one could even argue that some genres *depended* on anonymity for their existence. In truth, the stationers' dead authors had plenty of company; one might even say that they epitomized the facelessness of early modern authorship. This certainly would have made attributing authorship "intensely problematic," but most writers made no effort at all to rectify the situation; they seem rather to have perpetuated it. If early modern readers were profoundly "worried," even "possessed" by the question of attribution, the print industry seems to have ignored their concerns in egregious ways.

Because they were also consumers, however, those readers possessed a straightforward means of expressing their anxieties: they could vote with their pocketbooks. If consumers considered untrustworthy print to be valueless, one might reasonably expect sales figures to have declined as the print industry continued to subvert its own trustworthiness. Yet, the Stationers' almanacs once again suggest that the opposite is true. Almanac sales figures remained consistently strong throughout the eighteenth century. Indeed, the volume of sales for almanacs compiled by the dead authors significantly outstripped those for seventeenth-century almanacs, which usually bore the name of a living author on their covers. Consumers of print bought more almanacs precisely as authorial attribution became more problematic. If early modern readers had concerns about attribution, it appears that they also had other priorities which were more significant.

This glaring exception to Johns' rule requires us to consider whether one ought to treat "early modern readers" as a monolithic group with uniform priorities. Perhaps in the early modern era, as in ours, concerns about printed matter varied with the consumer's purposes, desires and perspective. It is significant in this regard that, while he critiques "fixity," Johns does not address Eisenstein's concept of "dissemination." Because Eisenstein alleges a role for fixity in the scientific revolution, Johns focuses on scholarly print, and uses scholarly consumers as the basis for generalizations about early modern print culture. Scholars evidently found early modern print insufficient for their purpose because it was not fixed, but it does not follow that non-scholarly consumers experienced the same problems. The majority of participants in early modern print culture were clearly not scholars, and so academic purposes would not have determined every writer's and reader's priorities. One can imagine consumers—merchants, perhaps, or politicians, or pleasure readers— whose purposes depended on the speed or extent of communication rather than its stability or authority. Such consumers would have found their activities greatly enhanced by the speed and extent of dissemination inherent in the early modern printing process.

Trust, from this perspective, depends not on authority but on sufficiency. For any consumer, a product is only problematic to the extent that it fails to serve his purposes. Scholarly consumers found early modern print to be insufficient for academic purposes because authorship was not attributable—because it lacked the fixity necessary to construct knowledge. If non-scholarly consumers found that same unstable, non-attributable print acceptable, they must have found it sufficient for their non-scholarly purposes. Trust, in other words, cannot be reduced to fixity, and non-attributable print could still be quite trustworthy as long as it was sufficient.

This functional trust could have been established by experience rather than attribution. In this regard, print would have resembled another locus of early modern chaos, the credit economy. J.G.A Pocock notes that the unpredictability of public stock values caused immense anxiety among early modern people. Stock trading was "seen as placing politics at the mercy of a self-generated hysteria (in the full sexist sense)." This forced eighteenth century thinkers to pursue "the stabilization of this pathological condition." In a world of imagination, authority became impossible to locate, but by focusing on outcome rather than source, Pocock's economic thinkers perceived a simple way to embrace systemic chaos:

> Defoe and others wrote about the conversion of "credit" into "opinion," Montesquieu about the conversion of "*crédit*" into "*confiance*". . . Such thinkers had recognized that, in the credit economy and polity, property had become not only mobile but speculative: what one owned was promises, and not merely the functioning but the intelligibility of society depended upon the success of a program of reification. If we were not to live solely in terms of what we imagined might happen—and so remain vulnerable to psychic crises like those of the Darien Scheme, the South Sea Bubble and the Mississippi Company—experience must teach us when our hopes were likely to be fulfilled, and *confiance* teach us that we might create conditions in which their fulfillment would be more likely.[49]

If early modern people could judge their new economic system by experience, they could surely have judged their new communication system in the same way. Using the criteron of sufficiency, Johns' scholars would still have found print untrustworthy because it failed in their experience. But other consumers could have had a different experience, and could have found print worthy of consistent, enthusiastic patronage. Trust took the form of experiential *confiance* as well as Johns' authorial "credit."

Judging by their buying habits, this was true for almanac consumers. Almanacs were as technically unstable as any print product, and more so in some respects. Yet almanac consumers seem to have had satisfactory experiences often enough to generate perpetually high levels of demand. One is tempted to extend these observations to a large number of non-scholarly genres. If annual demand was consistently high for almanacs during the eighteenth century, daily demand was equally insatiable for the ephemeral genres of newspapers, novels, plays, ballads and pamphlets. We know that the print culture, like the stock market, occasionally failed its participants, but high sales figures indicate that it did not normally do so. It seems that the texts purchased by early modern consumers proved sufficient for their purposes often enough to be considered desirable. The authorship of such print was certainly "retrospective, contingent, and contestable"; it was also often beside the point.

The Company as Author: Religious Politics

The prevalence of dead authors, pseudonyms, and anonymous compilers in British almanac production points away from personal responsibility for almanac content. In a word, the Stationers' Company—not its compilers—authored its own almanacs. Hired almanac makers may have written the actual copy and done the calculations, but the ideas they expressed had to fall within bounds set by the Company. If one is to evaluate the extent to which almanacs reflected contemporary norms, one must first assess the Company's motives for including or excluding certain opinions and ideas. The Company's motives can be reduced to two general categories: public constraints and internal preferences. Public constraints are not difficult to ascertain; the logic of the market, legal obligations, and monopoly status dominated the Company's behavior. The internal preferences of any group (let alone an early modern corporate body) are a bit more difficult to assess, but some evidence of Company members' political predilections—particularly those of the Court—does exist.

The English Stock monopoly was a two-edged sword. It generated lucrative profits, but the Company became legally liable for almanac content that ran afoul of the government. It also became financially responsible to the shareholders of the English Stock for products that failed to sell. The latter criteria—marketability—offers historians a high degree of assurance that almanacs' content reflected many of the mainstream beliefs, ideas, and norms of the English society that bought them. Financially speaking, the Company had no motive to include unpopular material and every motive to exclude it. If it did not pay, the Company excluded it; and if it did pay, somebody out there was clearly interested enough to buy it. Millions of individual decisions to buy an almanac affirmed that almanacs contained ideas which were feasible within prevailing worldviews, and largely consistent with popular understandings of the world.

Political constraints, however, ensured that the Company's almanacs contained only those mainstream beliefs that were acceptable to the government. As Capp has noted, official licensers usually ignored "ephemeral publications such as almanacs and ballads" during the seventeenth century, but "fearful of losing its privileges, the Company too operated an internal system of licensing in addition to that laid down by the state."[56] Even after the government ended direct censorship in 1695, to preserve the monopoly the Company had to play it safe. Given England's tumultuous politics under William and Anne, the Company could not afford to take a radical stance in favor of either party. It had to straddle as many factional lines as possible. Ecclesiastical positions defined many of those lines, so the Company's stance toward the Anglican Church was vital to its survival and success.

The Church had exercised direct official control of almanac content during the seventeenth century, but the system of almanac censorship by archiepiscopal chaplains "collapsed with the ruin of the Church in the early stages of the Revolution." Capp believes that the Company continued to submit its almanacs to clerical review until some undetermined point in the eighteenth century, but my sample of almanacs offers very little support for this notion. Of eighteen almanacs only one, *Olympia Domata*, carries a clerical imprimatur on its title page. This may have signified continued clerical monitoring, but it could also have been a marketing convention similar in function to the dead authors. As packaging designed to appeal to a niche market on the basis of nostalgia, political affiliation, or personal piety, an imprimatur could plausibly have indicated clerical approval of the one title only—and nominal supervision at that. Capp claims that Richard Gibson's 1712 edition of *Astrologus Britannicus* "appeared with blank spaces where material had been deleted," but the copy available for this study contains no such gaps.[57] No doubt this discrepancy means that these copies came from different impressions of the same edition. Regardless of this, deletions made during the editing process were not always ecclesiastical. The Company could easily have struck lines out of Gibson's copy on its own initiative. The evidence for systematic episcopal licensing of almanacs in 1711, then, is inconclusive at best. If the stationers did submit all of their almanacs systematically to comprehensive clerical review in 1711, they did so very quietly. It would be more plausible to suppose that any submissions to ecclesiastic authorities were limited, and motivated by commercial rather than political or religious considerations. Clerical censorship would have been a redundant formality in any case; the Company had too many motives for self-censorship to attribute deletions or alterations to clerical oversight. Political and economic motives would have been more than sufficient to steer the Company clear of controversial content without a bishop's guiding hand.[58]

Of course, avoiding controversial content does not equate to embracing all noncontroversial content. An internal bias could conceivably have led the stationers to overemphasize some conventional ideas or positions while excluding others. If internal biases had been strong enough, ideas could have been excluded in spite of potential profits and government approval. One ought to account as far as possible for any political or religious bias among the Company decision makers. Note that these two categories could not be entirely distinguished in early modern England; one's religious position informed and often defined one's politics, and a theological stance implied certain political inclinations.

It was politically significant, then, that the erstwhile bookseller John Dunton chose to define many of his fellow stationers by their religious affiliations. Of the seventeen stationers for whom Dunton cited religious-political affiliations, twelve were assistants who served on the Court between 1699 and 1710. Thus, if thirty-five men served on the Court of Assistants during the first decade of the eighteenth century, Dunton described the religious loyalty of one-third of the most prominent stationers.[59] Dunton may have been a mediocre merchant, but he was an astute judge of political influence. Like most Englishmen, he knew how to identify, and ingratiate himself to, potential patrons. He wrote his lists of acquaintances as part of an effort to cultivate favor among various groups, so one assumes that the image he constructed of the Stationers' Company was one which the Company itself sought to foster. Dunton's descriptions of its prominent members reinforced the Company's preferred public persona: an image of moderate Anglicanism.

Dunton identifies only two dissenters in his lists. Assistant Thomas Parkhurst served as Under Warden in 1689 and replaced William Phillips as Master in an emergency election held on 2 August 1703. Clearly a stationer of long-standing influence, he was also a nonconformist, "the most eminent Presbyterian Bookseller in the Three Kingdoms."[60] The bookseller Jonathan Robinson had been a liveryman since 1689, and he too was a dissenter. Dunton notes that although "he was very hospitable to the Sons of the Prophets in setting on the great Pot for 'em," his religious convictions "han't destroy'd the Goodness of his Humour, for his Temper is always easy and unruffled."[61] This remark indicates that Robinson was involved with "enthusiastic" low-church pietism of some sort, perhaps a millenarian sect. Two famous evangelical divines found his views congenial enough to sell their books through him: William Bates, "the politest" of his generation's evangelical Presbyterian preachers, and well known for his desire to see the Church of England "comprehend" the kingdom's nonconformists; and John Edwards, a "pungently Calvinist" Anglican writer who attacked latitudinarians such as John Locke as "Socinian" heretics.[62] Robinson never achieved an office above that of liveryman, but the patronage of these two eminent clergymen indicated a measure of social prominence. It is significant that while both clergymen were known for their Puritan theology, only Bates was a Presbyterian while Edwards remained firmly ensconced in the orthodox Anglican hierarchy. Even nonconformist stationers did not wish to stray too far from the official fold, at least not in public.

At the opposite end of the spectrum, Dunton named four high-church partisans. Printer/bookseller Thomas Bennett was elected Junior Renter Warden in 1701 and became an assistant in 1705. "Very much Devoted to the Church," Bennett was not a moderate and cultivated a reputation for printing "the most Eminent Conformists," particularly Robert South.[63] Ranked with Tillotson and Barrow as a great preacher, the witty South had been chaplain to Charles II and the Duke of York during the Restoration and served as prebendary of Westminster for over fifty years from 1663 to 1716. He bemoaned "the destruction of religion by 'Whigs and latitudinarians,'" and earned a reputation as the "scourge of [theological and political] fanaticism."[64] A cleric like South would have chosen his publisher with care, so one can be fairly certain that Bennett's sentiments aligned closely with the learned reverend doctor. Regardless, Bennett did well in the Stationers' Company, rising to Under Warden in 1711 and then Master after a mere four years on the Court.[65] Walter Kettleby became Upper Warden both in 1702 and 1703. He had served on the Court of Assistants for at least twenty years when Dunton called him "an Eminent Episcopal Bookseller" who was "pretty warmly dispos'd" in favor of Anglican conformity.[66] Charles Harper served as Under Warden in 1699 and Master in 1708. Dunton knew that he made "a considerable Figure in the Stationers-Company" and called him "a warm Votary for the high Church."[67] Daniel Brown must have been a prominent liveryman before 1705, but he figured primarily as a pirate of English Stock titles in Company records before his elevation to assistant on 25 March 1708. Dunton called Brown "a Sincere Lover of the establish'd Church," meaning that Brown favored the strict conformity of high-church Anglicans. Even so, Daniel Brown must have been the pragmatic sort; Dunton thought that in spite of his ecclesiastical opinions Brown's political "Principles [were] moderate enough." Not all exclusionist stationers wanted to exclude their customers.

The majority of Dunton's stationers stood at the congenial center of Britain's theological spectrum. The first of these, Brabazon Aylmer, was an old and trusted liveryman by 1705. Clothed in 1679, he served as a livery Stock-Keeper from 1700 to 1702. When the Tooke embezzlement scandal broke in 1702, Aylmer stepped in, supervised the warehouse until a new Warehouse-Keeper could be appointed, and received the "Thanks of the Court" at a meeting on 7 June 1703. Dunton called him "a very just and Religious Man," and many prominent clergymen agreed with the assessment.[68] The quintessential latitudinarian theologian and Archbishop of Canterbury, John Tillotson, chose Aylmer for his publisher. The books that Aylmer published for Tillotson included the works of Isaac Barrow, a famous preacher, pioneer of latitudinarian thought, and mathematical mentor to Isaac Newton.[69] Aylmer never achieved assistant status, but Tillotson's patronage and his personal reliability probably gave him close ties with the Stationers' Company leadership.

Aylmer's copublisher for Tillotson's works, William Rogers, did eventually become an assistant in 1708. Like Aylmer, he was well respected and had worn the livery since 1686. He had also taken Benjamin Tooke Jr. as one of his apprentices. His loyalties probably paralleled the latitudinarianism of Aylmer and Tillotson.[70] The venerable bookseller Edward Brewster was elected Upper Warden in 1687 and Master in the tumultuous year of 1689. He was Master again in 1690 and, in later years when he was out of office, he still stood in as substitute Master on occasion.[71] Dunton cited Brewster's publication of *The Practice of Piety* and *Doctrine of the Bible*, two classic explications of moderate Anglican orthodoxy, as evidence that Brewster was "a man of great Piety and Moderation."[72]

A younger man than Aylmer, Rogers, and Brewster, Nicholas Boddington took the Company's clothing in 1689. He became an assistant with Daniel Browne in 1708. By 1713 he had made Upper Warden, and he served as Master both in 1716 and 1717. In 1705, Dunton proved his ability as a talent scout by noting that Boddington made "a considerable Figure in the Parish where he lives," and that he dealt much in those emblems of solid Anglican orthodoxy, "Common-Prayer-Books."[73]

A longtime assistant like Kettleby, Henry Mortlock served twice as Under Warden in 1690 and 1691 before taking a turn as Master in 1696. Dunton reported that Mortlock enjoyed the patronage of "the great Doctor Stillingfleet Bishop of Worcester, and printed most of his Works."[74] Bishop Stillingfleet (like Tillotson and Barrow) was known for good preaching, good relations with dissenters, and moderate views—although he initiated "an intense and long-running polemic with John Locke over the supposed Socinianism of the *Essay Concerning Human Understanding*." As a favorite of both Charles II and Mary II, Stillingfleet would have made an enviable patron for any stationer and a fitting one for Master Mortlock. Dunton called liveryman Alexander Bosvile "a good Church-Man."[75] Samuel Lowndes, who served as Upper Warden in 1697 and 1698, was known simply as "Dr. Horneck's Bookseller."[76] Chaplain to the King, prebendary of Westminster, and preacher at the Savoy Chapel in London for most of the 1690s, Anthony Horneck's "fame as a preacher was matched by his reputation as a devotional writer and ascetic."[77] With Horneck in his corner, nobody could question Lowndes's credentials as a pious Anglican. Peter Parker put on the livery in 1669. He was a printer and an aggressive businessman who won concessions from the Company in 1675 to print Bibles at Oxford University. Dunton lists him simply as another stationer whose "Principles keep him intirely firm to the Interest and Religion of the Church of England."[78]

Two more stationers, Deputy Collins and John Heptinstall, rounded out the contingent of moderates. There is no evidence that Deputy Collins was ever apprenticed, freed, or clothed in the Company of Stationers, nor did he ever take an apprentice of his own. According to the Court book, however, Collins was appointed to the Court of Assistants along with three other stationers on 4 June 1705. Dunton knew him and called him simply "a moderate Church-Man."[79] John Heptinstall was clothed in 1689. Dunton noted that he was "a devout and constant Hearer of Doctor Pead." Aside from Heptinstall's devotion to him, nothing can be discovered of Pead—he is not named even on the Oxford and

Cambridge alumni lists—but Dunton says that he was "of the Church of England."[80] Robert Knaplock was destined for high office when Dunton mentioned him in 1705. The young bookseller became an assistant with the star class of 1708. He eventually served three consecutive terms as Under Warden from 1716 to 1718, two as Upper Warden from 1719 to 1720, and three as Master from 1722 to 1724. In 1705, however, he was known as the man who "printed Mr. Wesley's Defence of his Letter, &c." Dunton spent an unusual amount of effort excusing Knaplock for this youthful indiscretion, emphasizing that the bookseller was "no Dissenter." Despite this unfortunate association with unsavory enthusiasm, Dunton reassured his audience that Knaplock was "a very Sober Honest Man, and han't one spot in his whole Life, except it be the Printing that Malicious and Infamous Pamphlet." The vehemence with which Dunton minimized and otherwise rationalized Knaplock's brush with Methodism confirms that the Company feared even a hint of political deviance in their public image.[81]

If Dunton's list is proportionately representative, then moderate Anglicans comprised nearly two-thirds, high-church partisans about one-quarter, and nonconformists just over one-tenth of the Company's leadership. Even if Dunton skewed his list by 20 percent, moderate churchmen would still have held enough sway to ensure that their viewpoint could dominate almanac content. As it happens, the latitudinarian position also happened to be the safest political position of the day; so again, even if the moderates did not hold the supermajority indicated by Dunton's list, political prudence still bolstered their position. If Dunton's list is accurate, it accords well with the actual tenor of almanac content; if it is an exaggeration, it still indicates that the Stationers' Company recognized the utility of a latitudinarian image.

The Wardens' accounts bolster this assertion. The Company hired local clergymen to preach at their most significant annual feasts, Ash Wednesday ("Cakes and Ale") and the Election Feast ("Venison Feast"). The Wardens' account books show the faithful disbursal of £1 1s. 6p. "to the preacher for his sermon" at these feasts, and sometimes the lucky preacher is named. With no shortage of clerics in London, the Company's selection took on symbolic importance; its choice of preachers announced and reinforced the Company's official political stance, and offers the historian a useful way to judge the Company's political inclinations. On 8 February 1706, Under Warden Thomas Hodgkins paid the Ash Wednesday fee to Matthew Shorting. Shorting was an orthodox Anglican and headmaster of the Merchant Tailors' School.[82] At most, this choice would have been inoffensive, and perhaps it communicated solidarity with the larger guild community. In 1706, the Election Feast fee went to Offspring Blackall. Blackall was a more prestigious and also a more controversial choice than Shorting. He was an indisputably ortho- dox theologian. His vigorous controversy with John Toland over the au- thenticity of early Christian writings earned him the Boyle lectureship for 1700 at which he defended "The Sufficiency of a Standing Revelation." He was also closely tied to the post-Revolutionary establishment. Despite some accusations of Jacobitism, William III named him Chaplain to the King, and Queen Anne heard his sermons in 1704 and 1708 on the an- niversary of her accession. There was never any question, however, that Blackall was the epitome of a high-church Tory. His sermons regularly incurred Whig wrath, and his appointment as Bishop of Exeter in 1708 "greatly annoyed" low-church partisans. When the Company associated themselves with him, they risked similar annoyance among customers and their own low-church colleagues. Yet when it hired Blackall, the Company also signaled both its vigorous loyalty to Church and Queen, and its status as an audience fit for prestigious clerics.[83]

Two other clerics solemnized the stationers' feasts. Robert New- ton preached twice on Ash Wednesday. Rector of St. Augustine's at the Gate in London, Newton was unusually learned and a preacher of some repute. His presence probably reinforced the Company's preferred im- age of comfortable orthodoxy.[84] The stationers heard William Whitfield at their 1708 Election Feast. Whitfield was something of a local fixture in London: he served as canon of St. Martin's of Ludgate Church from 1691 to 1693, canon of St. Paul's from 1695 to 1709, canon of Canterbury until 1714, and then vicar of St. Giles Cripplegate until his death in 1717. From his career path, one supposes that people saw Whitfield as a learned man, well respected but unremarkable. Like Newton, his image would have reinforced the Company's politically inoffensive posture.[85] Taken as a whole, the Company's choice of clergymen signified its com- mitment to the established Church and to broad unity within that Church. The tacit image constructed by these choices—a generally mod- erate, although occasionally intense, Anglican orthodoxy—is consistent with the image conveyed by Dunton's list.

Notes

1. Letter from George Parker to the Court of Assistants, 2 August 1709 in Stationers, "Series 2–Box 33: Legal Papers (1680–1893)," 112.

2. Capp, *English Almanacs*, 45, 51.

3. Letter from George Parker to the Court of Assistants, 2 August 1709 in Stationers, "Series 2—Box 33: Legal Papers (1680–1893)," 112.

4. Note that because sheet almanacs were printed from an engraved copper plate, they were sometimes referred to as "plate almanacks." Stationers, "Court Book G; Fair Copy of Court Minutes 8 November 1697 to 6 May 1717," 57.

5. Voucher written by Tycho Wing to Thomas Simpson (Stationers' Company Warehouse-Keeper) 22 March 1743 in Stationers, "Series 1—Box C: 'Almanac Accounts and Advertisements,'" 98.

6. B. H. C., "Almanacs and Their Makers," *Notes and Queries: A Medium of Inter-Communication for Literary Men, Artists, Antiquaries, Genealogists, Etc.*, 9 June 1855.

7. Letter from John Baker Sr. to the Company of Stationers, 25 February 1771 in Stationers, "Series 1—Box C: 'Almanac Accounts and Advertisements,'" 98.

8. See the receipt signed by Wright on 12 June 1775 in Ibid.

9. Stationers, "Series 1—Box B: 'Almanac, Primer and Bible Printing: Infringement of Patents,'" 98, Folder 5.

10. R. Chambers, *Chambers's Book of Days, a Miscellany of Popular Antiquities in Connection With the Calendar Including Anecdote, Biography, & History, Curiosities of Literature and Oddities of Human Life and Character*, vol. 1 (Edinburgh: W. & R. Chambers, 1863), 13.

11. Capp, *English Almanacs*, 53–54.

12. Ibid., 243, 272. E. G. R. Taylor, *The Mathematical Practitioners of Tudor and Stuart England* (Cambridge: Cambridge University Press, 1954), 241.

13. A stationer named Watts paid £2 10s. on 16 September 1707 "for Advertisements in Almanacks." If one assumes that Watts's advertisement ended up in five almanacs, the fee for listing in one title would be 10s. An almanac maker earning a £5 fee plus free advertising would receive £5 10s. in value. Worshipful Company of Stationers, "Books in the Treasurer's Warehouse, 1663–1723," in *Records of the Worshipful Company of Stationers 1554–1920*, ed. Robin Myers, (Cambridge: Chadwyck-Healey, 1985) 84.

14. Stationers, "Court Book G; Fair Copy of Court Minutes 8 November 1697 to 6 May 1717," 57. To trace these negotiations, see the entries for 6 September, 6 November, 15 November, and 20 December.

15. Letter from Henry Hughes to the Stationers' Company, 11 November 1771 in Ibid.

16. Capp, *English Almanacs*, 304, 325, 327.

17. Research Library Groups, Inc. Eureka® English Short Title Catalogue, http://eureka.rlg.org [The British Library and ESTC/North America], "Swallow" (accessed 5 August 2003).

18. "Almanacs, English," in *Early English Books, 1641–1700: A Cumulative Index to Units 1–60 of the Microfilm Collection* (Ann Arbor, MI: University Microfilms, 1990); Ibid., "Fly".

19. Capp cites an earlier publication date in 1662, but the English Short Title Catalogue only carries editions dating from 1664. Capp, *English Almanacs*, 339, 378; R. L. G.'s Eureka English Short Title Catalogue, "Poor Robin".

20. Wiggins notes the dead authors as a distinguishing mark of eighteenth-century almanacs: "One of the major differences between almanacs of the eighteenth century and earlier is the way in which titles neither died with their author, nor were transferred to another author but rather continued as if the original compiler was immortal" (90–1). While he does not consider the implications of this anonymity for the content of his subject almanac, *Vox Stellarum*, his thesis does hint at a relationship between almanac content and "political realities," and notes occasional hints of an indirect "Government influence" and "an indirect form of control" (178–9, 183).

21. Capp, *English Almanacs*, 301, 355; R. L. G.'s Eureka English Short Title Catalogue, "Merlinus Anglicanus"; For the 1755 end date see the series of broadside advertisements preserved in Stationers, "Series 1—Box C: 'Almanac Accounts and Advertisements,'" 98.

22. Capp, *English Almanacs*, 303, 355; R. L. G.'s Eureka English Short Title Catalogue, "Culpepper Revived"; Taylor, *Tudor and Stuart*, 253. For the 1753 end date see the series of broadside advertisements preserved in Stationers, "Series 1—Box C: 'Almanac Accounts and Advertisements,'" 98.

23. Capp, *English Almanacs*, 377; R. L. G.'s Eureka English Short Title Catalogue, "Rose".

24. Capp, *English Almanacs*, 307, 360; R. L. G.'s Eureka English Short Title Catalogue, "Speculum Uranicum".

25. Perkins 1746 ended the series. Capp, *English Almanacs*, 324, 373; R. L. G.'s Eureka English Short Title Catalogue, "Perkins".

26. Capp, *English Almanacs*, 334, 378; R. L. G.'s Eureka English Short Title Catalogue, "Calendarium Astrologicum".

27. Capp considers Thomas White a pseudonymous author invented by the Company to capitalize on William White's successful series. While the later, longer-running *White* series is calculated for Toddington, Bedfordshire, this does not exclude the likelihood that Thomas was a relative of William. E. G. R. Taylor notes that advertisements in early editions of the Thomas White series contain self-descriptions of the author as a surveyor and dial maker. A ghost-writer would have used his own name in the advertisements, so the most plausible account must have Thomas taking up the series after William's death, and the Company retaining Thomas's name into the late eighteenth century. Capp, *English Almanacs*, 337, 378; Taylor, *Tudor and Stuart*, 275. For a record of

White's publication in 1778, see the "Financial Accounts of Almanacs" in Stationers, "Series 1—Box C: 'Almanac Accounts and Advertisements,'" 98.

28. Capp, *English Almanacs*, 378.

29. Quoted in Ibid., 45.

30. Letter of George Parker to the Court of Assistants, 2 August 1709 in Stationers, "Series 2—Box 33: Legal Papers (1680–1893)."

31. Capp, *English Almanacs*, 329, 378; R. L. G.'s Eureka English Short Title Catalogue, "Apollo Anglicanus"; Thomas Seccombe, "Saunders, or Sanders, Richard," in *The Dictionary of National Biography from the Earliest Times to 1900*, eds. Stephen and Lee, 817–18; Taylor, *Tudor and Stuart*, 227. See also M. H. Porter, "Saunders, Richard," Oxford Dictionary of National Biography (online edition) (accessed 22 Sep 2005), http://www.oxforddnb.com.

32. Capp, *English Almanacs*, 334, 378; R. L. G.'s Eureka English Short Title Catalogue, "Angelus Britannicus".

33. Capp, *English Almanacs*, 309; R. L. G.'s Eureka English Short Title Catalogue, "Astrologus Britannicus".

34. Williams expected his readers to be familiar with his personal history. His conversational tone and frankness must have added credibility to his prophecies: "Notwithstanding some Reports of my being Dead, it hath pleased Almighty God to let me live still; and also to enable Me to write this Almanack for the Year 1712 and the Astrological Judgments therein. The Truth is, it cannot be expected that I should write in this Annual way very many Years longer; in regard of my Great Age, being now in the Seventy Sixth Year thereof: but so long as God shall be pleased to enable me, I shall continue Writing in this manner hereafter." William Andrews, *Great News from the Stars: or, An Ephemeris for the Year 1712.* (London: Company of Stationers, 1711); Arthur Henry Bullen, "Andrews, William," in *The Dictionary of National Biography*, eds. Stephen and Lee, 409; see also R. L. G.'s Eureka English Short Title Catalogue, "News from the Stars".

35. Capp, *English Almanacs*, 311, 338, 378; Agnes Mary Clerke, "Wing, Vincent," in *The Dictionary of National Biography from the Earliest Times to 1900*, ed. Sir Leslie Stephen and Sir Sidney Lee (Oxford: Oxford University Press, 1921–22), 650–51; see also Bernard Capp, "Wing, Vincent," oxforddnb.com. R. L. G.'s Eureka English Short Title Catalogue, Taylor; *Tudor and Stuart*, 222, 258, 272.

36. Capp, *English Almanacs*, 242–43, 245–47, 334; Edward Irving Carlyle, "Tipper, John," in *The Dictionary of National Biography from the Earliest Times to 1900*, ed. Sir Leslie Stephen and Sir Sidney Lee (Oxford: Oxford University Press, 1921–22), 888; see also Bernard Capp, "Tipper, John," oxforddnb.com. E. G. R. Taylor, *The Mathematical Practitioners of Hanoverian England 1714–1840* (Cambridge: Cambridge University Press, 1966), 16–17, 38–39, 76, 91. In 1711, Tipper attempted a monthly serial called *Delights for the Ingenious* con-

sisting primarily of mathematical "enigmas" like those carried in *The Ladies' Diary*, but it lasted less than a year. A Court book entry of 5 June 1710 indicates that the Stationers' Company officially backed and partially funded the effort: "The Master likewise Acquainted the Court with Mr Tippers proposall of printing a Monthly Booke. The Question put whether the Court would meddle with it and it was agreed to try it a Month or two and give a Guinea for every Thousand that Shall be Sold."

37. Capp, *English Almanacs*, 230, 239–40, 320; Goodwin Gordon "Moore, Francis," 796; Francis Moore, *Vox Stellarum* (London: Company of Stationers, 1711). See also Patrick Curry, "Moore, Francis," oxforddnb.com.

38. Ben worked for Samuel Palmer at Bartholomew Close and John Watts at Wild's Court in Lincoln's Inn Fields. Benjamin Franklin, *The Autobiography of Benjamin Franklin*, ed. Leonard W. Labaree et al. (New Haven: Yale University Press, 1964), 96, 99; McKenzie, ed., *Stationers' Company Apprentices 1701–1800*, 258, 367.

39. Benjamin Franklin, *Poor Richard: The Almanacks for the Years 1733–1758*, ed. Limited Editions Club (New York: Paddington Press, 1976), 299.

40. Part of Jack Greene's prominence in the field of early American history derives from his convincing argument that imitation is a key to understanding early modern British colonial politics and culture. For a basic introduction to his work in this regard see Jack P. Greene, *Peripheries and Center: Constitutional Development in the Extended Polities of the British Empire and the United States 1607–1788* (New York: W. W. Norton, 1986); Jack P. Greene, *Pursuits of Happiness: The Social Development of Early Modern British Colonies and the Formation of American Culture* (Chapel Hill, NC: University of North Carolina Press, 1988); Jack P. Greene, "Empire and Identity from the Glorious Revolution to the American Revolution," in *The Oxford History of the British Empire*, ed. Peter James Marshall (Oxford: Oxford University Press, 1998), 208–230; Jack P. Greene, "Political Mimesis: A Consideration of the Historical and Cultural Roots of Legislative Behavior in the British Colonies in the Eighteenth Century," *American Historical Review*, 75, 2 (1969), 336–337. For other contributions to the social and cultural aspects of this phenomenon see Bernard Bailyn, *The Peopling of British North America: An Introduction* (originally published by Knopf: NY 1986 reprint Vintage Books: NY, 1988); David Hackett Fischer, *Albion's Seed: Four British Folkways in America* (Oxford: Oxford University Press, 1989). For specifically political manifestations of this phenomenon, see Jonathan Clark, *The Language of Liberty 1660–1832: Political Discourse and Social Dynamics in the Anglo-American World* (Cambridge: Cambridge University Press, 1994); Edmund S. Morgan, *Inventing the People: The Rise of Popular Sovereignty in England and America* (New York: W. W. Norton, 1988); John Grenville Agard Pocock, "Machiavelli, Harrington, and English Political Ideologies in the Eighteenth Century," *William and Mary Quarterly* 22, 4 (1965), 549–583; J. G. A. Pocock, *The Machiavellian Moment: Florentine Political Thought and the Atlantic Republican Tradition*

(Princeton, NJ: Princeton University Press, 1975); Jack Richon Pole, *Political Representation in England and the Origins of the American Republic* (Berkeley, CA: University of California Press, 1966). For a telling connection of American culture with the British consumer revolution, see Timothy Breene, "An Empire of Goods: The 'Anglicization' of Colonial America," *Journal of British Studies*, 25, 4 (1986), 467–499.

41. Titles and brand names were not the only mimetic elements in Franklin's almanac repertoire. "Jonathan Swift's assault on Partridge was imitated in detail by Benjamin Franklin in the 1730s. Franklin, like 'Bickerstaff' predicted and then announced the death of a prominent [American] almanac maker, Titan Leeds, and carefully refuted the victim's attempts to prove that he was still alive." Capp, *English Almanacs*, 275–76.

42. Neil McKendrick, John Brewer, and John Harold Plumb, eds., *The Birth of a Consumer Society: The Commercialization of Eighteenth-Century England* (Bloomington, IN: Indiana University Press, 1982). The importance of commercial context in the history of print is also emphasized in John Feather, "The Commerce of Letters: The Study of the Eighteenth Century Book Trade," in "The Printed Word in the Eighteenth Century," special issue, *Eighteenth-Century Studies* 17, no. 4 (1984), 405–424.

43. "If we seek the intellectual origins of the revolution in consumption we will find them in the 1690s. If we seek the wide acceptance and application of these ideas we have to move into the second half of the eighteenth century." Neil McKendrick, "The Consumer Revolution of Eighteenth-Century England," in *The Birth of a Consumer Society: The Commercialization of Eighteenth-Century England*, ed. Neil McKendrick, John Brewer, and J. H. Plumb (Bloomington, IN: Indiana University Press, 1982), 13.

44. "It must be stressed that every aspect of leisure that I touch upon in the rest of this chapter is aided in its development and commercial organization by print, whether it is the circus or landscape gardening, horse-racing or concert-going." J. H. Plumb, "The Commercialization of Leisure in Eighteenth-Century England," in *The Birth of a Consumer Society: The Commercialization of Eighteenth-Century England*, ed. Neil McKendrick, John Brewer, and J. H. Plumb (Bloomington, IN: Indiana University Press, 1982), 266–73.

45. "The avowed purpose was to proclaim one's ability constantly to improve on the old and the inherited, and of course, to swell the demand for what was new and modern." Neil McKendrick, "Introduction," in *The Birth of a Consumer Society: The Commercialization of Eighteenth-Century England*, ed. Neil McKendrick, John Brewer, and J. H. Plumb (Bloomington, IN: Indiana University Press, 1982), 2.

46. Elizabeth Eisenstein, *The Printing Press as an Agent of Change: Communications and Cultural Transformations in Early-Modern Europe* (Cambridge: Cambridge University Press, 1979), 71–88, 113–26; Johns, *Nature of the Book*,

10–11, 13–14, 19, 21, 31.

47. Johns, *Nature of the Book,* 291.

48. Ibid., 137.

49. Ibid., 30–31.

50. Ibid., 58.

51. William Shakespeare, "Two Gentlemen of Verona," in *The Complete Works of Shakespeare,* ed. David Bevington (New York: HarperColllins, 1992), 2. 1.164.

52. Feather's thoughts on this topic are worth quoting in full: "Since the middle of the sixteenth century the chain of production and distribution has become ever more complex, and the demands and practices of the producers of books have often intervened rather than merely interposed themselves between author and reader. To the literary scholar this intervention is the most familiar when it has been the deliberate or accidental cause of change in the artistic intentions of the author. The perspective of the historian is a little different [because he is] less concerned with textual niceties" Feather, "Commerce & Letters," 405.

53. Daniel Defoe, "An Essay on the Regulation of the Press," in *Freedom of the Press: Six Tracts 1698–1709* (New York: Garland Publishing, 1974), 1.

54. John Brewer, "Commercialization and Politics," in *The Birth of a Consumer Society: The Commercialization of Eighteenth-Century England,* ed. Neil McKendrick, John Brewer, and J. H. Plumb (Bloomington, IN: Indiana University Press, 1982), 200.

55. Ibid., 217.

56. Defoe, "A Letter to a Member of Parliament, Shewing the Necessity of Regulating the Press," 40.

57. Capp, *English Almanacs,* 47.

58. Ibid., 240, 240n.

59. Authoritative work on legal strategies to control the press fails to mention Church oversight. After 1695, the primary functional stricture on press content seems to have been Jacobitism, not heresy. If it couldn't be construed as Jacobite propaganda, the government was both helpless and uninterested. If it could be construed as Jacobite propaganda, the government was interested but usually still restricted in its options. See especially John P. Feather, "From Censorship to Copyright: Aspects of the Government's Role in the English Book Trade 1695–1775," in *Books and Society in History,* ed. Kenneth E. Carpenter (New York: R. R. Bowker, 1980), 173–198; John P. Feather, "The English Book Trade and the Law 1695–1799," *Publishing History* 12 (1982), 51–57.

60. I used the Court book entries for 19 July 1700, 14 July 1702, 4 June 1705, 25 March 1708, and 27 September 1710, and eliminating redundancies identified thirty-five distinct names: William Phillips, Richard Simpson, Samuel

Sprint, Edward Brewster, Robert Scott, Robert Clavell, Henry Mortlock, Richard Chiswell, Walter Kettilby, Thomas Parkhurst, William Shrewsbury, Charles Harper, Thomas Hodgkins, Robert Roberts, Robert Andrews, Robert Clevell, John Place, Samuel Roycroft, George Copping, Israel Harrison, Deputy Collins, Henry Bonwick, Thomas Bonnott, Edward Darrell, Daniel Browne, William Rogers, Timothy Goodwin, Nicholas Boddington, Richard Mount, John Sprint, John Lawrance, Robert Knaplock, Freeman Collins, John Baskett, and William Freeman.

Samuel Lowndes (one of the stationers named by Dunton) was on the Court in 1699, but his name disappears from the roster by Election Day 1700.

61. Dunton, *Life and Errors*, 281; Stationers, "Court Book G; Fair Copy of Court Minutes 8 November 1697 to 6 May 1717."

62. Dunton, *Life and Errors*, 282; McKenzie, ed., *Stationers' Company Apprentices 1641–1700*, 143; McKenzie, ed., *Stationers' Company Apprentices 1701–1800*, 298, 421.

63. J. A. I. Champion, *The Pillars of Priestcraft Shaken: The Church of England and Its Enemies, 1660–1730* (Cambridge: Cambridge University Press, 1992), 111–12; Alexander Balloch Grossart, "Bates, William, D. D.," in *The Dictionary of National Biography*, eds. Stephen and Lee, 1319–20; Charles John Robinson, "Edwards, John," in *The Dictionary of National Biography from the Earliest Times to 1900*, ed. Sir Leslie Stephen and Sir Sidney Lee (Oxford: Oxford University Press, 1921–22), 539–40; John Venn and J. A. Venn, eds. *Alumni Cantabrigienses, a Biographical List of All Known Students, Graduates and Holders of Office at the University of Cambridge, from the Earliest Times to 1900; Part I, from the Earliest Times to 1751*, vol. 2, Dabbs-Juxton (Cambridge: Cambridge University Press, 1927), 88; Venn and Venn, eds., *Alumni Cantabrigienses*, vol. 1, *Abbas-Cutts,* 107; John Walsh and Stephen Taylor, "Introduction: The Church and Anglicanism in the 'Long' Eighteenth Century," in *The Church of England C. 1689–1833*, ed. John Walsh, Colin Haydon, and Stephen Taylor (Cambridge: Cambridge University Press, 1993), 43, 52. See also Stephen Wright, "Bates, William," oxforddnb.com.

64. Dunton, *Life and Errors*, 283; McKenzie, ed., *Stationers' Company Apprentices 1701–1800*, 402; Stationers, "Court Book G; Fair Copy of Court Minutes 8 November 1697 to 6 May 1717."

65. Champion, *Pillars*, 100; Joseph Foster, ed., *Alumni Oxonienses: The Members of the University of Oxford, 1500–1714: Their Parentage, Birthplace, and Year of Birth, with a Record of Their Degrees*, vol. 2, *Labdon-Zouch* (Wiesbaden, Germany: Kraus Reprint Limited, 1968), 1391; Mark Goldie, "John Locke, Jonas Proast and Religious Toleration 1688–1692," in *The Church of England C. 1689–1833*, ed. John Walsh, Colin Haydon, and Stephen Taylor (Cambridge: Cambridge University Press, 1993), 154; Alexander Gordon, "South, Robert, D. D.," in *The Dictionary of National Biography from the Earliest Times to 1900*, ed. Sir Leslie Stephen and Sir Sidney Lee (Oxford: Oxford University Press, 1921–22), 683–85; Gordon Rupp, *Religion in England, 1688–1791*, ed. Henry and

Owen Chadwick, Oxford History of the Christian Church (Oxford: Clarendon Press, 1986), 41, 513, 514. See also Burke Griggs, "South, Robert," oxforddnb.com

66. For an example of Brown's piracy, see the Court book entry for 7 September 1702 referring to his illegal "epitome" of *Foxe's Book of Martyrs*, one of the English Stock's religious patents. Dunton, *Life and Errors*, 284; McKenzie, ed., *Stationers' Company Apprentices 1701–1800*, 403; Stationers, "Court Book G; Fair Copy of Court Minutes 8 November 1697 to 6 May 1717."

67. Dunton, *Life and Errors*, 417; McKenzie, ed., *Stationers' Company Apprentices 1701–1800*, 403, 416.

68. Dunton, *Life and Errors*, 287; McKenzie, ed., *Stationers' Company Apprentices 1701–1800*, 402–3.

69. Dunton, *Life and Errors*, 282; McKenzie, ed., *Stationers' Company Apprentices 1701–1800*, 414; Stationers, "Court Book G; Fair Copy of Court Minutes 8 November 1697 to 6 May 1717."

70. Foster, ed., *Alumni Oxonienses*, vol. 1, *Aban-Kyte* (Wiesbaden, Germany: Kraus Reprint Limited, 1968), 78; Goldie, "John Locke," 152, 163–64, 170; John Henry Overton, "Barrow, Isaac," in *The Dictionary of National Biography from the Earliest Times to 1900*, ed. Sir Leslie Stephen and Sir Sidney Lee (Oxford: Oxford University Press, 1921–22); Rupp, *Religion in England*, 36–37, 311. Regarding the senior clerics mentioned in this section, Jonathan Clark notes, "The polemics in which Restoration Anglicans like Isaac Barrow, Robert South, Edward Stillingfleet and John Tillotson engaged had a powerful influence into the early nineteenth century. They achieved a 'synthesis of scriptural revelation and human reason' which maintained their writings in print and which was relied on as an established premise by large numbers of their coreligionists. If eighteenth century Anglican preaching often limited itself to moral exhortation, it has been suggested, it was because a belief in the achievement of this generation of divines freed later generations from certain at least of the possible dogmatic challenges to their position." Clark, *Language of Liberty*, 34.

71. Dunton, *Life and Errors*, 284; McKenzie, ed., *Stationers' Company Apprentices 1641–1700*; McKenzie, ed., *Stationers' Company Apprentices 1701–1800*, 417; Stationers, "Court Book G; Fair Copy of Court Minutes 8 November 1697 to 6 May 1717," 57.

72. See, for example, the Court book entries for July 1707 when Brewster served as acting Master in Edward Darrell's absence.

73. Dunton, *Life and Errors*, 283; McKenzie, ed., *Stationers' Company Apprentices 1701–1800*, 402.

74. Dunton, *Life and Errors*, 286; McKenzie, ed., *Stationers' Company Apprentices 1701–1800*, 403, 421; Stationers, "Court Book G; Fair Copy of Court Minutes 8 November 1697 to 6 May 1717."

75. Dunton, *Life and Errors*, 286; McKenzie, ed., *Stationers' Company Apprentices 1701–1800*, 403, 419.

76. Dunton, *Life and Errors*, 287.

77. Ibid., 289; McKenzie, ed., *Stationers' Company Apprentices 1701–1800*, 402.

78. Foster, *Alumni Oxonienses*, 747; John Spurr, "The Church, the Societies and the Moral Revolution of 1688," in *The Church of England C. 1689–1833*, ed. John Walsh, Colin Haydon, and Stephen Taylor (Cambridge: Cambridge University Press, 1993), 132; Sir Leslie Stephen, "Horneck, Anthony," in *The Dictionary of National Biography from the Earliest Times to 1900*, ed. Sir Leslie Stephen and Sir Sidney Lee (Oxford: Oxford University Press, 1921–22), 1261–62; Venn and Venn, *Alumni Cantabrigienses*, 409. See also W.R. Ward, "Horneck, Anthony," oxforddnb.com.

79. Blagden, *Stationers' Company: A History*, 197–99; Dunton, *Life and Errors*, 307; McKenzie, ed., *Stationers' Company Apprentices 1701–1800*, 413.

80. Dunton, *Life and Errors*, 325; Stationers, "Court Book G; Fair Copy of Court Minutes 8 November 1697 to 6 May 1717."

81. Dunton, *Life and Errors*, 329; McKenzie, ed., *Stationers' Company Apprentices 1701–1800*, 422.

82. Dunton, *Life and Errors*, 293; McKenzie, ed., *Stationers' Company Apprentices 1701–1800*, 403–4.

83. Venn and Venn, *Alumni Cantabrigienses*, 69. See also Andrew Starkie, "Blackall, Offspring," oxforddnb.com.

84. John Henry Overton, "Blackall, or Blackhall, Offspring," in *The Dictionary of National Biography from the Earliest Times to 1900*, ed. Sir Leslie Stephen and Sir Sidney Lee (Oxford: Oxford University Press, 1921–22), 579–80; Venn and Venn, *Alumni Cantabrigienses*, 160. See also Andrew Starkie, "Blackall, Offspring," oxforddnb.com.

85. Charlotte Fell-Smith, "Newton, Benjamin," in *The Dictionary of National Biography from the Earliest Times to 1900*, ed. Sir Leslie Stephen and Sir Sidney Lee (Oxford: Oxford University Press, 1921–22), 365–66; Foster, *Alumni Oxonienses*, 1066; Venn and Venn, *Alumni Cantabrigienses*, 253. See also Fell-Smith rev. Robert D. Cornwall, "Newton, Benjamin," oxforddnb.com.

86. Stationers, "Wardens' Accounts 1663–1728," 76.

๑ Chapter Six ๑

Almanacs and Printer Patronage

*T*he Company's choice of printers for its almanacs was an integral component of its corporate authorship. As mentioned earlier, the artisinal process of early modern printing made the printer something of an interpreter as well as a producer of texts. Printed texts often reflected the printer's perceptions as well as his skill, so if control of almanac content helped construct the Company's public image, it would have been important to select trustworthy printers. As one would expect, Company leadership did distribute English Stock almanac patronage in distinct patterns that revealed their priorities. Insofar as they were all stationers in good standing, one assumes that almanac printers conformed to the religious-political norms explored above. Beyond such generalities, however, the Company's almanac printers do not fall into a discernable partisan category. The patterns of English Stock patronage evidently had little to do with tight control of almanac content. Rather, those patterns reveal a set of communal priorities specific to the Company itself. The assistants used their almanac patronage to fulfill practical obligations to the community they governed. They used patronage to bolster the Company's financial, social, and political interests—and to care for its constituents. As artifacts as well as texts, English Stock almanacs reflected the Company's communal values.

Multiple Sheets, Multiple Printers

Although the name of a single printing firm appeared on every title sheet, no book almanac was the work of a lone printer. During the seventeenth century, Capp notes that it was common practice to have different printers produce the calendar and the ephemeris portions of book almanacs.[1] This practice continued into the eighteenth century. The 1712 editions of *Swallow* and *Speculum Uranicum* carry the names of different printers for the two sections, but even the almanacs that list a name only on the title page usually have notable differences in typeface and quality between their calendars and prognostications. This division of labor extended beyond the two sections to include individual sheets within the sections. Cyprian Blagden notes that in the late seventeenth century the Company "often employed more than one printer for the same almanack." He surmises that while a printer's name usually appeared on the title page, this "denoted the printer of the first two sheets; the third sheet—and in 'sorts,' the half sheet—was very often printed by another whose name seldom appeared."[2]

The logic of piracy and patronage fostered the development of this piecework system. A single stationer printing all the sheets for an almanac could—and often did—print extra copies to sell on the sly. Assigning even one sheet out of four to a different printer complicated such endeavors. Under the piecework system, collusion among two or three different stationers would have been required to assemble illicit supernumerary copies. If the Warehouse-Keeper—who assigned all work for the English Stock—successfully kept the sheet assignments secret, would-be pirates would have had to seek out the printers of companion sheets in a relatively open manner. This, of course, placed the Warehouse-Keeper in a uniquely privileged position. By keeping his printers in the dark as to which of their colleagues was printing the other sheets for a given almanac, he alone possessed the power to pirate the Company's products. Ben Tooke ran into trouble for doing exactly that. His crucial mistake was using the Company's money to pay for his supernumerary copies; indeed, it was not the actual piracy of English Stock titles that outraged the stockholders in 1702 but the embezzlement of Stock funds. A moderate amount of piracy may well have been, at least tacitly, one of the perks of the Warehouse-Keeper's position.

A post-Tooke Warehouse-Keeper could have avoided Tooke's fate either by raising his own capital to pay surreptitiously for unauthorized sheets or by negotiating explicitly with the printers and promising them a share of his illicit profits. Despite these possible abuses, the piecework system effectively reduced the potential scale of piracy. Instead of multiple printers with independent access, the power to pirate under the piecework system resided with a single salaried agent. Aside from this advantage, subdividing English Stock projects benefited the Company in another way by increasing its patronage. It did not take a natural philosopher to figure out that the more sub-tasks one created, the more favors one had to divvy out.

For these reasons, piecework quickly became standard practice for the English Stock during the eighteenth century. As early as 1737, the stationer Sam Idle earned £35 9s. for printing the title sheet of *Moore's Almanack*, sheet B of *Wing*, sheet C of *Coley*, and half of sheet C plus three wood cuts for *Ladies' Almanack*. Clearly it was not just the third sheet that was being assigned to a separate printer. All sheets—the title sheet, sheet B, and sheet C—went into separate contracts. With sheets from four different almanacs going to this single printer, it seems logical to assume that all titles were dissected in the same way. This was undoubtedly the case by the 1770s. A series of 1779 receipts to John March, Randall Brown, H. Goldney, and Harris Hart indicate that printers were receiving much smaller contracts by this time—usually just one sheet. The account book for 1778 confirms this, listing forty-six printers paid for work on just nineteen titles.[3] However, without this sort of direct evidence it is difficult to tell whether or not piecework was a universal practice in the early eighteenth century.

The stationers undoubtedly thought of almanac production in terms of sheets rather than whole books during their negotiations with George Parker in 1717. The Parker agreement indicates that printers thought of almanac sheets as units of monetary value, not literary continuity, and that the Company saw piecework as insurance against piracy. In addition, the Court minutes during this period mention numerous lawsuits against almanac pirates, but none of the complaints referred to supernumerary copies. Rather, the Court was preoccupied with the inclusion of calendars "which are the Companys Coppy" in unauthorized—but largely original—ephemeredes. This suggests that the structural safeguards of sub-tasking were indeed firmly in place by the time the 1712 editions were printed.

The only refinement in the system during the eighteenth century was the atomization of contracts as more and more printers enjoyed smaller and smaller bits of the almanac printing pie. Whereas printers in the 1770s could expect to print one or two almanac sheets, printers in the 1700s probably printed three or four sheets apiece. It is reasonable to assume, then, that for the early eighteenth century, the printer named on one almanac's title sheet was also the anonymous printer of sheets B or C for three or four other almanacs. Even though the Warehouse-Keeper's account books for the early eighteenth century are unavailable, one can safely assume that every almanac printer during that period got his name on at least one title sheet every year.

Place-Seekers and Place-Holders

Almanac printing meant good money for those printers lucky enough to get a contract. According to Blagden, the English Stock during the 1670s paid 3s. 4d. for a ream (150 sheets) of rubricated print, and 2s. 6d. for black-only printing. Five decades later, Sam Idle earned twice those rates: 7s. 6d. per ream for a rubricated title sheet, 8s. per ream for the more intricate sheet B, and 6s. a ream for a black-only sheet C. Use of Company-provided paper minimized overhead costs so that the £35 Idle earned from his three-month contract was almost all profit.

Small wonder, then, that the Court received a steady stream of employment requests. While the Warehouse-Keeper had day-to-day control of hiring and work distribution, the Court retained final jurisdiction and would-be English Stock employees went to the assistants to make their case. Average stationers viewed English Stock patronage as a perk of membership, and they were not bashful about claiming it. Ichabod Dawkes was already on the Company payroll in 1703 when he made a request in person, "desiring that hee may have more work from the Company." The assistants duly "ordered that the Store Keepers doe appoint some more worke to Mr Dawks," but it is uncertain whether there was any extra work available.[4] However, after John Hayes (the old printer of *Olympia Domata*) died in late 1705, Dawkes began printing that title sheet. Other printers chose to write letters rather than appeal in person on a Court day. The printers Wright and Gill in Abchurch Lane wrote:

> As Members of this worshipful Company, we beg Leave to sollicit such a share of your Favors, as you shall judge may be for the Interest of the Company.
>
> We flatter ourselves from the many Years we have been in Trade, and the Extensiveness of our Connections, that it is in our Power to execute any Orders you should be inclined to favour us with in such a Manner as may be a Credit to us, and give you the fullest Satisfaction.[5]

Similarly, John Johnson wrote:

> The Death of Mr. John Oliver having occasioned a Vacancy for a Part of the Company's Printing I beg leave to remind you that I have been upward of twenty one Years upon the Livery and have not yet been honoured with any Work for the Company and hope to bee considered on the present Occasion.[6]

It is telling that Oliver's death opened a "vacancy" in an otherwise un-available set of places. Both letters indicate that stationers thought of English Stock work as a lifetime gift—sometimes even a hereditary hold-ing—for those lucky enough to get it.

Evidence indicates that the idea of lifelong contracts was not just a perception. An exceptional number of printers held contracts for the title sheets of the same almanac for decades at a stretch. They seem to have held their contracts almost by right, and quite often that right seems to have become hereditary. The Horton family printed the *Angelus Britan-nicus* title sheet for 24 years from 1677 to 1701. The Wilde family held *Apollo Anglicanus* for 35 years from 1701 to 1736, *Fly* for forty-four years from 1708 to 1752, and *Great News from the Stars* for 70 years from 1694 to 1764. The Maxwell family printed *Calendarium Astrologicum* for 15 years from 1659 to 1674. The Clark family printed *Apollo Anglicanus* for thirty years from 1670 to 1700. Cambridge University printer John Hayes printed a raft of almanac titles from 1680 until his death in 1706. William Bowyer, followed by his son, printed *Poor Robin* for seventy-two years from 1703 to 1775. The Everingham family printed *Speculum Uranicum* for 27 years from 1685 to 1712 and *Woodhouse* for twenty-seven years from 1680 until at least 1707. The Dawkes family printed *Olympia Do-mata* for 28 years from 1708 to 1736. The Parker family printed *Olympia Domata* for 35 years from 1738 to 1773. The White family printed *White* (the compiler was evidently no relation to the printers) for 29 years from 1661 to 1690. The Roberts family printed John Partridge's *Merlinus Lib-eratus* for at least 27 years from 1687 to 1714. Richard Brugis printed *Perkins* for 20 years from 1707 to 1727. Thomas Hodgkins printed *Rose* for 37 years from 1679 to 1716. Henry Clark printed *White* for 18 years from 1691 to 1709. The Janeway family printed *Culpepper Revived* for 14 years from 1708 to 1722.[7] Once he acquired a contract with the Com-pany, a stationer could reasonably expect to earn a guaranteed minimum amount every year for the rest of his tenure in the trade.

This is not to say that printers had anything resembling legal title to their Stock work. They held their jobs at the pleasure of the Court, and there were a number of ways to lose one's patronage. The most obvi-ous way to do this was to insult the Court outright. On 3 June 1700 "Mr. Onely the Printer comeing to bind an Apprentice [behaved him-self] very contumatiously to the Court." The assistants immediately voted "That hee be noe more Employed by the Stock Keepers of this Company nor have any Worke for the future upon Account of the English Stock"—heavy consequences for a moment's pique. A printer also risked his En-

glish Stock job if his slipshod work harmed the Company's public reputation. In 1704, the Court summoned Benjamin Mott to explain "the
printing the Church Catechism for the Company wherein is a mistake
in the printing of the Apostles Creed by inserting the Resurreccion of the
Dead whereas itt ought to be the Resurreccion of the body." Mott
"owned there was a mistake in the printing of the Church Catechism
with Scripture proofes but he alledged twas so in the coppy hee had
from the Hall." Although "hee promised the mistake should bee rectified
by the reprinting thereof [the Court] Ordered that the printing of the
Church Catechism bee removed from Mr Mott."[8] Sometimes, heads had
to roll. Curiously, a final way to lose access to English Stock patronage
was to become an assistant. On 3 November 1701, the Court.

> Ordered that noe printer or printers whilst he or they is Master
> Warden or Stockeeper shall for the future during the time of
> his being soe have any more or other of the Stockworke of the
> said Compy than hee or they had before their comeing into
> such office.

Patterns of Patronage

As with most selfless acts, this decision by the Court to recuse itself from Stock contracts had a practical rationale. The Court had more
urgent uses for its patronage than enriching assistants. To become a
prominent stationer, one had to be rich in the first place, and control of
patronage meant power—a commodity considerably more valuable to
those wealthy men than a few more bits of gold. Considerable obligations to the Company accompanied that power, and the assistants de-
ployed their patronage to meet those requirements.

The foremost of these responsibilities was charity. The original rationale for the English Stock monopoly was to provide a pension for
the guild's poor, disabled, and aged—and in this era before bureaucratic
government doles, it would have been hard to overestimate the importance accorded to this private safety net by the average stationer. In addition to quarterly pensions issued at Charity Courts, the Company distributed a "Weekly Charity of Bread & Money" and housed a number of
aged pensioners on the grounds of Stationers' Hall.[9]

Even at regular meetings, a considerable amount of the assistants'
time went to charitable issues. At most monthly meetings (as well as at
quarterly Charity Courts) the Court found itself voting to increase or
decrease individual pensions "in respect of their poverty," to admit a

new pensioner or move an existing pensioner into a better room vacated by death, or to evaluate exceptional petitions. A few examples will suffice. "Upon reading the peticion of Henry Nye a liveryman of this Company above 20 years since" on 20 December 1711, the Court ordered "that he have 30 s. out of the poores Box which was given him accordingly." On 18 December 1702, the assistants "Ordered that Robert Chown and Elienor Foster Pencioners of this Company have five Shillings apiece added to their pentions in respect of their poverty." On 4 February 1712, the Court was "moved to Consider the present poverty and Circumstances of Mr. Abott Swaile who has paid his livery and Renterwardens fine many yeares since." The assistants voted to help Swaile set up shop, granting him the "Summe of £5 to be applyed for him in the buying of Bookes in order to putt him in to some business for Supporting himself and the Same to be placed to the Charity account in the next pencion papers." In a poignant example of personal relations transcending official connections, the assistants "voluntarily subscribed" £10 8s. out of their own pockets to help the son of their recently deceased Beadle on 3 May 1703.[10] Despite several instances of self-serving mismanagement before and hence, the assistants who governed the Stationers' Company during the early eighteenth century seem to have honestly viewed themselves as stewards of their community; the lower sorts depended on the assistants' vigilant custody, and both parties seem to have taken this quite seriously.

In extraordinary circumstances, association with the stationers might mean more than simply access to the Company dole; it also facilitated access to government emergency funds and to support from a broad network of colleagues. When disaster struck William Bowyer and his family on 29 January 1713, the promising young printer received massive private and public aid largely because of his status as a Company liveryman. Fire incinerated the Bowyer shop and home that Thursday night, killing an elderly uncle and reducing the premises to a heap of smoldering ashes. The Bowyer family lost everything but the nightclothes on their backs. The damage—including household possessions, book stocks, paper stocks, and printing equipment—totaled a staggering £5,146. Overnight— and in the middle of winter—the Bowyers had gone from riches to rags.

Potentially vulnerable to starvation and exposure, an eighteenth century Englishman in this situation discovered just how much his society valued him. The Bowyers, evidently, were valuable indeed. At the request of the Lord Mayor himself, the Queen issued a "Royal brief" endorsing gifts to compensate the loss. The brief, which was read from the pulpits of every English parish, reinforced the government's approval of productive subjects like William who "acquired considerable substance, and lived in a creditable manner."[11] In an act of charity that might puzzle their descendants, strangers from across the kingdom gave the Bowyers £1,377. Gratis. Perhaps more impressive, several prominent liverymen initiated a private subscription that nearly matched this anonymous largesse. Subscription lists name the entire Court of Assistants and most of the prominent liverymen as contributors. The Earl and Countess of Thanet, Lord Weymouth, Lord Guilford, the University of Cambridge, and Bowyer's friend George Stanhope—Dean of Canterbury—pitched in as well. Private gifts totaled £1,162. In a matter of weeks, the charity of friends, colleagues, patrons, and the kingdom at large had made good over half of the Bowyers' material loss.[12]

In light of such substantial benefits, it is not surprising to find nonstationers—usually nonmember employees or friends of stationers—looking to the Company to secure their financial security. Almanac compiler Henry Coley bought Company bonds worth £400 and was presumably allowed to do so because of his long-standing services to the English Stock. In 1710, Assistant Knaplock proposed that "a Gentlewoman . . . friend of his above fourscore Years of Age" be allowed a £40 annuity upon paying £200 into the Company treasury. His fellow assistants would only agree to a £30 payment, but they evidently found the request itself unremarkable. They were used to captaining an economic lifeboat.[13]

The Company's charitable effort (or should it be called an insurance program?) extended beyond English Stock profits to include English Stock patronage. As the case of William Bonny indicates, the Court of Assistants often leveraged its patronage power to help it fulfill charitable obligations. Every stationer knew that, despite his honesty and industry, Bonny was cursed with extraordinarily bad luck. He had lost his first business in London in the early 1690s, but before he went under the Company attempted to keep him afloat by assigning him two almanac contracts: Bonny printed the 1689–91 editions of *Merlinus Anglicanus* and the 1690–91 editions of *Great News from the Stars*. In 1695, the lapse of the Licensing Act rendered printing legal outside of London, and Bonny helped initiate the provincial press by establishing a shop in Bristol. No sooner was he back on his feet than, true to form, he went "stark blind." Had Providence not intervened, however, the Court could have taken great satisfaction in its adroit use of patronage to assist a fellow stationer. By making Bonny an almanac printer, they had kept him off the Company poor rolls and in his shop for nearly five years. The arrangement had yielded multiple benefits, preserving Bonny's pride as a self-sufficient artisan while causing him to contribute to Company profits rather than draw on its charity funds.[14]

The logic of this work-welfare tactic accounted for the disproportionate number of female names appearing on almanac title pages. Widows were the Company's responsibility until they married or died, and many women chose to keep their husbands' presses running rather than live on a meager Company allowance. This was a winning idea from both the Court's perspective and from the widow's. An industrious widow could earn a far more comfortable income for herself than the Company dole could hope to provide, and fewer widows on Company charity meant fewer burdens on the stationer community's resources. As with Bonny, the logic of charitable patronage was evident: providing guaranteed annual work to a widow benefited the Company even more than it benefited her.

A large number of widows lived by this system from the 1650s onward. John Dawson printed *Vaux Speculum Anni* beginning in 1642, and after his death Gartrude Dawson continued printing the title from 1653 to 1666. The Company granted her three other almanac contracts as well: *Daniel* in 1651, *Philo-mathematicus* from 1651 to 1653, and Thomas Nunne's *An Almanack* from 1661 to 1662. The Company's decision to increase Gartrude's patronage after John's death reinforces the idea that the Court had charity in mind when it distributed its patronage. Margaret White printed *White* from 1680 to 1683, after her husband Robert White held the contract and before Bernard White—presumably her son—took it over.

Sarah Griffin, probably widow of Edward, printed *Rose* from 1656 to 1673, as well as the 1687 edition. She also printed William Andrews's *De rebus caelestibus* in 1658. David Maxwell printed *Calendarium Astrologicum* for six years from 1659 to 1665, and his widow Anne continued printing it until at least 1674—possibly as late as 1679. The Company also assigned her *Woodhouse* from 1667 to 1674. Andrew Clark printed *Apollo Anglicanus* from 1670 to 1680, and his widow Mary continued printing it from 1681 to 1699 or 1700. Mary Clark also printed *Goldsmith* from 1692 to 1695 and Vincent Wing's broadside almanac from 1682 to 1693.

Robert Everingham printed *Speculum Uranicum* from 1685 to 1706 and *Merlinus Anglicanus* from 1702 to 1708. His widow, Elinor, printed *Speculum Uranicum* from 1708 to 1712 and *Merlinus Anglicanus* until 1716. She also received William Turner's short-lived *An Almanac* for the duration of its production from 1708 to 1710. After Richard Janeway Jr.'s death in 1714, Elizabeth Janeway continued printing *Angelus Britannicus* and *Culpepper Revived.* Although she had been printing the prognostication section of *Swallow* for some time, the Company transferred *Swallow*'s title page to Elizabeth from John Barber in 1716. She also received a contract for *Tate's and Brady's Psalms* in 1724.

The number of widows who printed almanacs indicates that charity played a large role in distributing English Stock patronage. That all but a few of these widows received multiple contracts after their husbands died reinforces this notion. The Company took every opportunity to keep its members, and particularly its most vulnerable members, in business rather than on its dole. Almanac contracts served as a sort of insurance against unemployment for individual stationers and against unemployment payments for the stationers as a community.[15]

Elizabeth Janeway's case demonstrates both the insurance rationale behind much Company patronage and the tacit hereditary ownership that developed around some English Stock contracts. Elizabeth's husband, Richard Janeway Jr., was a printer working out of Whitefriars. He received two almanac contracts at the turn of the century—the title sheets of *Angelus Britannicus* in 1701, and *Culpepper Revived* in 1707 following John Hayes's death—and he continued to print both until his own death in 1714. He also acquired the contract for the ephemeris section of *Swallow* in 1712. When he died, Elizabeth took over all of his contracts. The year 1715 marked the end of the *Angelus Britannicus* series, but the Company promptly replaced it with *Swallow*'s title sheet so that she never had fewer than two full contracts. After Elizabeth died sometime in mid-1725, her Stock contracts and her two wards—an apprentice named Edmund Hall, and her youngest son, James—went to printer Thomas Burdett.

Giving the titles to Burdett could have served two purposes—compensating him financially for the sudden burden of two extra apprentices, and keeping the almanac contracts in a kind of trust for young James. The system worked well for James Janeway. He completed his apprenticeship on 7 July 1730 and set up shop in his parents' old neighborhood of Whitefriars. The 1731 editions of *Swallow* and *Culpepper Revived* were probably among the first sheets to leave the young yeoman's press. James printed *Culpepper Revived* until it was discontinued in 1737 and *Swallow* until 1740. The Company took responsibility both for Elizabeth and for the well-being of the two young men she left behind. Like stationer widows and invalids, stationer orphans and wards were part of the family, and the Company maneuvered its resources to ensure their transition to productive membership in the trade.[16]

A similarly pragmatic approach accounts for the number of Company tenants printing Company almanacs. Robert Everingham had printed almanacs since 1678, the same year he began renting a house from the Company. For the rest of his life, he printed the title pages for at least two almanacs every year, beginning with *Perkins* and *Woodhouse*. Although his contract for the title page of *Perkins* went to another printer in 1684, he received the contract for *Speculum Uranicum* that same year. Similarly, Robert Roberts began renting one of the Company's houses on Ave Maria Lane at some point around 1680. He printed his first almanac title page, Partridge's *Merlinus Liberatus*, in 1687. Everingham rented his house for £28 per year and Roberts rented his for £32. If the average income from almanac printing ranged from £20 to £30, the Company was essentially subsidizing its own renters by giving them a guaranteed annual income equal to their annual rent. As with the stationer widows, this added up to a win-win situation. The Company ensured that its renters would not default while also causing them to contribute to Company profits. The renters, on the other hand, received guaranteed housing.[17]

The Company's thinking in this respect became especially apparent when its tenants were also widows. For instance, when Robert Everingham died in 1706 (suddenly it seems—he was still taking and freeing apprentices in 1705), his widow Elinor continued renting their house from the Company. She also continued printing Robert's almanac titles, *Speculum Uranicum* and *Woodhouse*, until 1712 when both were discontinued. The Company ensured that she had other almanac jobs, however. Elinor printed the title page for *Merlinus Anglicanus* until 1716, as well as William Turner's short-lived *An Almanac* for the duration of its production from 1708 to 1710. She either died or went out of business in late 1717 or early 1718, and her two remaining apprentices were turned over to other printers—but despite her status as an elderly widow, she was always able to pay her rent.[18]

The same can be said of Mary Harrison, whose husband James died suddenly in 1768—leaving her with five children, a printing business, and seven years worth of back rent due to the Stationers' Company. Evidently James had worked for the English Stock before his death—he was, after all, a Company tenant—but without a doubt, Mary printed almanacs for the Stock after his death. She acquired a new set of almanac-specific type (presumably symbols for the zodiac and planets), and at one point labor costs forced her to raise the price of a set of school primers by 1s. per ream. By July 1770, she had made good on four years worth of back rent. Her bill for printing was figured on a ledger next to her husband's debt, and the Warehouse-Keeper deducted set portions from her cash fee. The Company won two ways in Mary's case: it recouped rent that would have been completely lost otherwise, and it kept six mouths off of the common dole. In this way, the Harrison case exemplified the insurance function of stationer patronage; while every case was unique, the Court sought to deploy its patronage to secure both the welfare of individual stationers and the Company's financial interests.[19]

A notoriously fine line, however, divided financial interests from political interests. Many of the widows employed by the English Stock were merely building on patronage their husbands had acquired by other means. Similarly, the Company owned a limited number of properties; deciding which stationers to take as tenants must have involved some measure of internal politics, particularly since those properties seem to have been largely subsidized. Indeed, it would be difficult to say which came first—the patronage or the charity. The question of how one or the other was acquired in the first place remains obscure in most cases, but evidence of internal favoritism exists for a few. The most prominent of these was Company tenant Robert Everingham. Everingham gained his freedom from master Ralph Davenport in 1661. In a show of personal endorsement, John Macocke—a future Master of the Stationers' Company—joined Davenport in vouching for Robert's freedom. The young yeoman printed his first almanacs, *Perkins* and *Woodhouse*, in 1679—the year after his mentor Macocke became Upper Warden of the Court. Doubtless, Macocke had some say in the decision to award patronage to his protégé. *Perkins* went to other printers, but Everingham received the contract for the *Speculum Uranicum* title sheet in 1685 and continued printing it and *Woodhouse* for twenty more years. He also printed the title sheet for *Merlinus Anglicanus* from 1702 to 1705. After he acquired the favor of a prominent stationer as an apprentice, Everingham found himself with a guaranteed income for the rest of his life.[20]

Family heritage played as significant a role in Stock patronage as political connections. Almanac printers such as Richard Brugis and Ichabod Dawkes probably acquired their initial contracts at least in part as a tribute to their families' long tradition in the trade. Ichabod was the same Dawkes who petitioned the Court for more Stock work in 1703, so he was already working for the Company when he received the contract for *Olympia Domata*'s title sheet after John Hayes's death. There is very little to indicate why the Court granted his request, or even hired him in the first place, except that Ichabod represented the third generation of his family in the trade. Ichabod Dawkes's father, Thomas, was reputed to be "a printer of some celebrity in his day." At some point over three generations' time, this prominent family managed to get a foot in the warehouse door. As demonstrated above, once a family acquired a contract it was likely to stay employed for as long as it was in the business, so Ichabod benefited from family connections at least as much as his own industriousness.

Richard Brugis also grew up in the printing trade. His father, Henry, had been a master printer since at least 1660 when he took his first apprentice, and young Richard received the Company's freedom by patrimony in 1691 or 1692. He had established his own shop, probably on Jewin Street, by 1704, and he entered the livery on 3 November 1707. He began printing the *Perkins* title sheet in 1706 following the death of its previous printer, Elizabeth Leach, and continued printing it for two decades. In the absence of other information, one speculates that the assistants saw Brugis in the context of his family heritage and his professional potential. He represented the second generation of a family which had been contributing to the trade for at least fifty years. Also, Brugis had a reputation as a "high flyer," and the assistants probably found it worthwhile to endorse a winner. It was probably not a coincidence that Brugis received the *Perkins* contract a year before he was called to the livery. Like Ichabod Dawkes and countless other Stock contractors, Brugis's patronage expanded over time; he added the title sheet for *Calendarium Astrologicum* to his list in 1723.[21]

Brugis's case indicates that one can sometimes construe the Court's patronage as a sign of its approval for, even sponsorship of, promising talent within the trade. If so, the assistants' prophecies of prominence often proved quite accurate. Like Brugis, Thomas Hodgkins began printing his first almanac—*Rose*—in 1679, shortly before he was admitted to the livery in 1682. Hodgkins became an assistant on 8 April 1700; he served as Under Warden in 1704 and 1705, and as Upper Warden in 1709. Along with this high station, his gift of two guineas to the Bowyer fund indicates that he had accumulated more than the average amount of wealth by the end of his life.[22] The Company's tenant Robert Roberts fit in the same category as Hodgkins. He entered the livery before Hodgkins in 1679, but his name did not appear on an almanac title sheet until Partridge's *Merlinus Liberatus* for 1688. Like Hodgkins, however, Roberts received his assistantship in 1700, and he held the *Merlinus Liberatus* contract until his death in 1708.

Although no record of Thomas Wilmer's apprenticeship exists, he was a fairly prominent member of the Company during the early eighteenth century. Admitted to the livery on 14 March 1703, he was wealthy enough to fine for Renter Warden on 23 March 1711 and to subscribe the considerable sum of three guineas—more than Assistant Hodgkins—to the Bowyer relief fund in 1713. He took his first apprentice in 1704 and freed his last apprentice in 1733. The Company's widely respected Stock-Keeper, Joseph Collyer, chose to bind his son Thomas to Wilmer in August 1704. Three years later, Wilmer received the contract for *Astrologus Britannicus*. The Court was probably doing its Warehouse-Keeper a favor in this case; the patronage gave Collyer a means of ensuring his son's good standing with a wealthy master. As it turns out, *Astrologus Britannicus* was a short-lived almanac title; it was scrapped after the edition for 1712, the same year that young Thomas Collyer gained his freedom. Wilmer printed no other almanacs after *Astrologus Britannicus*, so this bit of the Company's patronage appears to have been directed more to Collyer than to himself. By doing favors for its Stock-Keeper, the English Stock would have reinforced his sense of reciprocal obligation and reduced his incentive for fraud. No less important, however, the Company also acknowledged and supported one of its more successful young members.[23]

William Bowyer—the printer whose house burned in 1713—was another of the Court's prescient picks. He received the freedom of the Company in 1686. He set up his own printing shop in 1699 and did so well for himself that the Court considered him fit for the livery a year later. Like Hodgkins, Bowyer received his first almanac contract—the title sheet of *Poor Robin*—shortly after appointment to the livery; but unlike most printers, the Bowyer firm held that same contract for a staggering seventy-two years. Bowyer enjoyed considerable patronage outside of the Company as well—particularly that of prominent centrist clerics—and he allied himself to one of the trade's most venerable families by marrying Ichabod Dawkes's sister, Dorothy. As noted earlier, Bowyer's reputation carried him through a personal disaster that would probably have ruined a less-prominent man. Alexander Pope's decision to trust the first edition of his *Iliad* to Bowyer just two years after the fire affirmed the Court's acumen in endorsing Bowyer's career.[24]

If anything, John Barber's success was more pronounced than Bowyer's, and more deeply intertwined with almanac patronage. Barber started out working for Hannah Clarke, a widow and recipient of the Company's charitable patronage. Hannah began printing *White* in 1691, the same year that her husband, Henry, died. Yet her firm foundered under poor management for several years. While John Barber was still an apprentice, Hannah must have recognized his precocious talent and arranged for him to replace her current manager, Mr. Sedgwick. Bar-

ber's master, George Larkin, freed him in 1696. Hannah joined Larkin
in formally vouching for Barber's freedom and immediately hired him
to manage her shop. Despite his relative lack of experience, the business
boomed under young Barber's direction, and word quickly got around
that Hannah had made a very savvy choice.[25] Barber entered the livery
in October 1705, and his name first appeared on the *Swallow* almanac in
1708. Like his friend, William Bowyer, he also enjoyed non-Company
patronage from early on in his career. Barber maintained close connections with the prominent Tory literati of the day—including Dean Swift,
Alexander Pope, and Lord Bolingbroke—and he and Tooke received a
patent as printers to the Queen in 1713 during the Tory ascendancy. One
story has it that after the House of Lords found a pamphlet printed by
Barber to be objectionable, he avoided prosecution by calling in the
copies and replaced the offending page with a paragraph composed
for him by Bolingbroke. He became printer to the City of London in
March 1709, Renter Warden for the Company of Stationers on 26 March
1710, and he and his partner, Benjamin Tooke Jr., were proprietors of
the newspaper of record, the *London Gazette*, by 1711. Not surprisingly,
Barber "acquired considerable opulence" during the ensuing decade, despite being a "Jacobite in principle." He managed to come out on top
in the South Sea debacle and became wealthy enough to serve as Alderman of the Castle Baynard ward in 1722. He served as Sheriff of London in 1730, and as Lord Mayor two years later. Dean Swift evidently
influenced him to choose one Matthew Pilkington as chaplain during his
mayoralty, and he left several hundred pounds each to Bolingbroke,
Pope, and Swift.

Barber's career demonstrates rather vividly the Court's rationale
for patronizing promising young printers: they just might become powerful. When talented, ambitious, or well-pedigreed tradesmen achieved
their proper station in life, one might reasonably have expected them
to remember who helped them get there. It was in the Court's interest to
invest in future allies. Then too, one could argue that the entire stationer community had an interest in seeing its most gifted members rise
to leadership positions both within and outside the Company structure.
Wealth was a prerequisite for entering any position of influence, so the
Company used its patronage to foster the careers of likely young lead-
ers. It is perhaps telling that Alderman Barber established his public
reputation by working for widow Clarke. Such close familiarity with the
challenges faced by a widow printer would have impressed him early on
in his career with the difference an English Stock contract like the *White*
almanac could make to someone in Hannah's position. He doubtlessly

understood the charitable rationale that dictated much of the Company's patronage policy. When widow Elizabeth Janeway received Barber's contract for *Swallow* in 1716, he had assumed a relatively prominent place in society. One wonders whether the transfer was the Court's idea or his own.[26]

In a similar manner, the case of James and Mary Roberts ties the Company's use of patronage to endorse successful young stationers together with its financial motives of securing an income for its widows and tenants. James and Mary were both related to Robert Roberts, who appears frequently in the previous narrative. Robert's sons, James and Jasper, acquired the Company's freedom by patrimony on 11 July 1692 and 5 June 1695, respectively. Both had earned sufficient wealth to enter the livery within four years of their freedoms. Indeed, James was able to subscribe a whopping five guineas to the Bowyer relief fund. Jasper's chances at wealth met an untimely end when he died sometime before 9 February 1707 on which day his widow, Mary, took her first apprentice. Clearly, Mary intended to carry on Jasper's business in her own right, and she and brother-in-law James are undoubtedly the "M. and J. Roberts" who appeared on the title page of *Great Britain's Diary* in 1710. The last two editions of *Merlinus Liberatus* (those for 1709 and 1714) also bore their imprint. James's name appeared by itself on *Great Britain's Diary* after 1714, so Mary had either died or remarried in 1713. As the widow of a liveried printer, Mary would have been an obvious candidate for Company patronage. A second-generation printer with the considerable wealth that accompanied skill and good business sense, James appeared destined for an influential role in the trade, so he too fit the profile for an English Stock contractor. True to his potential, he became Under Warden in 1727 and served as Master in 1729 and 1730—and decades later, Nichols described him as "a printer of great eminence."

But James and Mary were the only printers to appear jointly on an almanac title page in the early eighteenth century. As *Merlinus Liberatus* had been in the Roberts family for decades, both of them had a plausible claim to the contract. The case for patronage seems all the more compelling when one finds that James had located his business and residence in Stationers' Court itself since at least 1710. Like his father, he was both a successful young liveryman and one of its tenants; he was also the sole surviving heir of a prominent trade family. He was just the sort of leading stationer who would be expected to look out for the welfare of Company widows like his sister-in-law Mary. All of the themes that run through Company patronage converged in this pair—charity, widowhood, tenancy, family heritage, and leadership potential. Granting patronage jointly to James and Mary Roberts made sense in almost every way it was possible to make sense from the Company's perspective.[27]

Almost every way; but external politics influenced the Company's patronage decisions nearly as much as internal politics. Two almanac printers, John Hayes and Elinor James, embodied the political utility of patronage. Hayes became printer to the University of Cambridge in 1669. The two universities possessed official privileges that competed with those of the English Stock, which included the right to print almanacs. Rather than allow competing almanacs to enter the market (legally for once), the Company assigned a large amount of its almanac work to Hayes; this included the title sheets for *Culpepper Revived, Fly, Olympia Domata, Swallow,* and *Wing.* When Hayes died in late 1705, the Company sent a delegation to negotiate with the university. They paid Cambridge £210 a year to forego its almanac privilege, and the Company redistributed the Stock work that had belonged to Hayes to stationers closer to home. The Company chose to pay in cash what it had previously paid in patronage, but the effect was the same. Both cash fees and patronage subsidies could be used to preserve the English Stock monopoly.[28]

In granting almanac work to Thomas James, the Court of Assistants sought preservation of another kind. One expects that when James acquired his freedom on 16 December 1661, he mostly knew what he was getting into—but there was no way he could have known what he was bargaining for when he married Elinor. Elinor James gave birth to at least three sons and two daughters; she also produced a steady stream of political invective, advice, and commentary—much of it (but surely not the majority) in print. Everyone in London knew about "that She-State-Politician, Mrs. Elinor James." She was, to put it mildly, "a very extraordinary character, a mixture of benevolence and madness." Unpredictable, forceful, and utterly self-assured, Elinor wrote from 1685 to 1715, producing a raft of broadside pamphlets on everything from the proper behavior of journeyman printers to the evils of Jacobitism. She corrected, praised, and advised each monarch in turn, claiming to have walked to Windsor and back on foot for the sole purpose of "telling Charles II of his faults." She prayed piously for Queen Anne, and accused George I of plotting to set fire to London and of going to church to "to talk to his daughter and play with dogs and puppies" rather than worship. In 1689—shortly after giving birth to her daughter, Elizabeth—Elinor served a short stint in Newgate prison "for dispersing scandalous and reflective papers." There is no evidence that this surprised anyone. She took an apprentice in 1704, several years before her husband's death, and considering herself qualified to give "advice to all printers in general"—she carried on his business when he finally passed away.

It is no accident that the English Stock gave almanac contracts to Thomas James for thirty-three consecutive years from 1678 to 1711. He printed the title sheets to the *Bowker* almanac from 1678 to 1684, the *City and Countrey Chapmans Almanack* from 1684 to 1692, the *Chapman's and Traveler's Almanack* from 1693 to 1695, and *The English Chapmans and Travelers Almanack* from 1696 to 1710. He was assigned the title sheet to *Calendarium Astrologicum* in 1704, and continued to print it until 1710. After his death in 1711, Elinor continued publishing *Calendarium Astrologicum* until 1715, when presumably she died. Thomas James may have been "a man that reads much, knows his business very well, and is extremely obliging to his customers," but his personal characteristics alone could not have merited the sort of consistent, even insistent, patronage he received from the Company. Unlike many of the long-term almanac printers, the James firm did not print the title sheet for the same almanac year after year, but while the titles may have shifted, he always received a full share of work. One gets the impression that the Company wanted to ensure that Thomas never lacked for a piece of the English Stock pie. Yet he had no influential sponsor like Robert Everingham's John Macocke, and he was not especially influential in his own right: for most of his career he was evidently not even wealthy enough to be called to the livery.

The Company's solicitude makes sense only when one considers Elinor James's penchant for attack-dog editorials. Even the formidable Elinor might have thought twice before biting the hand that fed her family. Since Thomas's status as husband likely carried little weight by itself, the Court probably knew that he needed a bit of leverage to dissuade her from publishing her most outrageous screeds. Like everyone else, Elinor would have known that the Company avoided political controversy at all costs. So when she came up with a particularly controversial opinion, Thomas could argue that publishing scandalous pieces would reflect poorly on the Company—thus jeopardizing their English Stock patronage. Conversely, Elinor's energies may have proven useful when the Company wished to endorse or condemn something without direct attribution. In giving almanac work to Thomas, the Stationers' Company insured itself against Elinor's somewhat unpredictable activism, and bought some measure of control over a potential political liability.[29] The intent in this case as in the others was to maximize benefit for the stationer community by deploying resources to secure the Company's social, legal, economic, and political interests.

Notes

1. Capp, *English Almanacs*, 43.

2. Blagden, "Distribution of Almanacks," 112.

3. Stationers, "Series 1—Box C: 'Almanac Accounts and Advertisements.'"

4. Dawkes's request on 6 December 1703 reminded the Court to catch up with the status of its English Stock patronage. (Recall that this was right after the Ben Tooke scandal, so several liverymen were temporarily supervising the warehouse.) The Court "Ordered that the Storekeepers bee desired to give by the next Court day an account of the Store worke of the company that are in the severall printers hands and how they are severally employed and in what work." Stationers, "Court Book G; Fair Copy of Court Minutes 8 November 1697 to 6 May 1717," 7.

5. Letter from Wright and Gill to the Court of Assistants, 3 January 1775 in Stationers, "Series 1—Box M: English Stock and Irish Plantation (Manor of Pellipar) 1673–1964," 104, Folder 9.

6. Letter from John Johnson to the Court of Assistants, 17 January 1776 in Ibid.

7. The length of various contracts can be judged by tallying citations in the index entry "Almanacs, English" of R. L. G.'s Eureka English Short Title Catalogue, an on-line database.

8. See entries for 27 March 1704 and 8 April 1704 in Stationers, "Court Book G; Fair Copy of Court Minutes 8 November 1697 to 6 May 1717," 57.

9. Stationers, "Series 1—Box M: English Stock and Irish Plantation (Manor of Pellipar) 1673–1964," 104, Folder 6.

10. Stationers, "Court Book G; Fair Copy of Court Minutes 8 November 1697 to 6 May 1717," 57.

11. These briefs were fairly common. An Order in Council issued after Anne's death in 1714 reestablished Bowyer's brief as still in effect. Money was contributed via "parsons, vicars, curates, churchwardens, [and] overseers of the poor" and forwarded via the Church hierarchy to London. A study of such briefs, perhaps in conjunction with private subscriptions, might offer insight into the intricate dynamics of an embattled religious establishment, a nascent capitalist economy, private associations, and an increasingly formalized bureaucracy. Nichols, *Literary Anecdotes*, 74–75.

12. Ibid., 50–64.

13. See the entries for 25 March 1704 and 24 May 1704 in Stationers, "Wardens' Accounts 1663–1728," 76. See also entries for 5 March 1705 and 6 November 1710 in Stationers, "Court Book G; Fair Copy of Court Minutes 8 November 1697 to 6 May 1717," 57.

14. Dunton, *Life and Errors*, 329.

15. Information associating names with almanac titles and publication dates can be found in the index entry "Almanacs, English," R. L. G.'s *Eureka English Short Title Catalogue*, an on-line database. For relationships, first names, and occasionally widow status look in McKenzie, ed., *Stationers' Company Apprentices 1641–1700*; McKenzie, ed., *Stationers' Company Apprentices 1701–1800*.

16. "Almanacs, English," R. L. G.'s *Eureka English Short Title Catalogue*, "Janeway"; McKenzie, ed., *Stationers' Company Apprentices 1701–1800*, 59, 192; Plomer, *Printers and Booksellers*, 170.

17. A helpful study would determine the number of company renters who received this kind of subsidy via the English Stock. Unfortunately, the Renter Wardens' records do not extend back beyond 1851. Prior to that year, one relies on the Court books to cite renters' names when their leases came due for renewal. This is how we know that Roberts and Everingham were Company tenants. On 3 February 1701 "Mr Everingham" was listed as a Stationers' Company tenant. The entry for 2 March 1702 states that "Mr Everingham a Tenant to the company came into Court and acquainted them that if they would repair his Roofe he would take a Lease thereof for 21 years at the same Rent he now holds it being 28." The Court attempted to put the expense of repairs onto its renter on 24 March 1702 when it "Ordered that upon Mr Everingham's putting the said house in good Repaire att his own Charge the said Mr Everingham is to have a Lease thereof for 21 years at 26 l. [illeg.] Ann." The deal was finally closed on 13 April 1702 when "Mr Everingham attending without was called in and acquainted by the Court. . . . But Mr Everingham not approving thereof upon debate of the matter it was Resolved That the Company would put the said house in good repair att their Charge And that Mr Everingham should have a Lease thereof under the same Rent as formerly vizt att 28 l p ann."

A similar account exists for the Roberts family. On 3 February 1701 the Court "Orderd that Mr. Roberts House to be put in repaire and that he have a new Lease thereof from the Company for One and twenty Years to commence from Lady day att the same Rent hee now pays being 32 per Annum to be paid Quarterly (side note: house in Ave Maria Lane). Roberts's widowed daughter-in-law was also listed as a renter in a 24 March 1702 minute, noting a "Lease from the Company to Mrs Mary Roberts of two houses fronting the Hall now laid into one dated 9th February 1701 for 21 years from Lady day last att 32 l. And was Sealed with they Common Seals in open Court."

Note that since twenty-one years is the standard length of the Company's leases, I calculated the dates of Everingham's and Roberts's original leases by subtracting twenty-one years from their lease renewal dates. Stationers, "Court Book G; Fair Copy of Court Minutes 8 November 1697 to 6 May 1717."

18. "Almanacs, English," R. L. G.'s *Eureka English Short Title Catalogue*, "Everingham"; McKenzie, ed., *Stationers' Company Apprentices 1641–1700*, 45, 54, 104; McKenzie, ed., *Stationers' Company Apprentices 1701–1800*, 119, 401.

19. See "Mrs. Harrison's Account with the Worshipful Company of Stationers" and the unsigned, undated letter to the Court of Assistants mentioning Harrison in Stationers, "Series 1—Box M: English Stock and Irish Plantation (Manor of Pellipar) 1673–1964," 104, Folder 6, Folder 9.

20. "Almanacs, English," R. L. G.'s Eureka English Short Title Catalogue, "Everingham"; McKenzie, ed., *Stationers' Company Apprentices 1641–1700*, 45, 54, 104; McKenzie, ed., *Stationers' Company Apprentices 1701–1800*, 119, 401.

21. "Almanacs, English," R. L. G.'s Eureka English Short Title Catalogue, "Brugis"; McKenzie, ed., *Stationers' Company Apprentices 1641–1700*, 24; McKenzie, ed., *Stationers' Company Apprentices 1701–1800*, 54; Negus, "Private List," 303; Worshipful Company of Stationers, "Calls of the Livery: 22 June 1606 to 5 November 1765," in *Records of the Worshipful Company of Stationers 1554–1920*, ed. Robin Myers (Cambridge: Chadwyck-Healey, 1985) 41.

22. "Almanacs, English," R. L. G.'s Eureka English Short Title Catalogue, "Hodgkins Thomas"; McKenzie, ed., *Stationers' Company Apprentices 1641–1700*, 174, 402–3; McKenzie, ed., *Stationers' Company Apprentices 1701–1800*, 80–1, Stationers, "Calls of the Livery: 22 June 1606 to 5 November 1765", 41; Stationers, "Court Book G; Fair Copy of Court Minutes 8 November 1697 to 6 May 1717," 57.

23. Dunton, *Life and Errors*, 296; McKenzie, ed., *Stationers' Company Apprentices 1701–1800*, 381; Nichols, *Literary Anecdotes*, 62; R. L. G.'s Eureka English Short Title Catalogue, "Wilmer"; Stationers, "Calls of the Livery: 22 June 1606 to 5 November 1765", 41; Stationers, "Court Book G; Fair Copy of Court Minutes 8 November 1697 to 6 May 1717," 57.

24 Nichols, *Literary Anecdotes*, 71, 76n.

25. "Almanacs, English," R. L. G.'s Eureka English Short Title Catalogue, "Barber John"; Dunton, *Life and Errors*, 330; McKenzie, ed., *Stationers' Company Apprentices 1641–1700*, 30.

26. Nichols, *Literary Anecdotes*, 72–75, 485, 535; Worshipful Company of Stationers, "Check Books 1648–1805," in *Records of the Worshipful Company of Stationers 1554–1920*, ed. Robin Myers (Cambridge: Chadwyck-Healey, 1985), 75; Tooke and Barber, "The London Gazette, 4 October to 6 October 1711"; Tooke and Barber, "The London Gazette, 11 October to 14 October 1712." For Barber's clothing date, see the entry for 1 October 1705 in Stationers, "Court Book G; Fair Copy of Court Minutes 8 November 1697 to 6 May 1717," 57.

27. "Almanacs, English," R. L. G.'s Eureka English Short Title Catalogue, "Roberts, James", "Roberts, Mary"; Dunton, *Life and Errors*, 325, McKenzie, ed., *Stationers' Company Apprentices 1641–1700*, 102, 142; McKenzie, ed., *Stationers' Company Apprentices 1701–1800*, 296, 404, 422–23; Negus, "Private List," 290; Nichols, *Literary Anecdotes*, 62; Plomer, *Printers and Booksellers*, 255; Worshipful Company of Stationers, "Apprentice Memorandum Books 1724 to 1920,"

in *Records of the Worshipful Company of Stationers 1554–1920*, ed Robin Myers (Cambridge: Chadwyck-Healey, 1985) 33; Stationers, "Court Book G; Fair Copy of Court Minutes 8 November 1697 to 6 May 1717," 57.

28. See the entries for 2 March 1702 and 3 December 1705 in Stationers, "Court Book G; Fair Copy of Court Minutes 8 November 1697 to 6 May 1717," 57. For the complex details behind Hayes's status see Blagden, *Stationers' Company: A History*, 199–203. For the Company's decision to pay off Cambridge, see Blagden, "Thomas Carnan," 30; Capp, *English Almanacs*, 240.

29. Negus, "Private List," 305n; Bertha Porter, "James, John," in *The Dictionary of National Biography from the Earliest Times to 1900*, ed. Sir Leslie Stephen and Sir Sidney Lee (Oxford: Oxford University Press, 1921–22), 650–51; Dunton, *Life and Errors*, 334; "Almanacs, English," R. L. G.'s Eureka English Short Title Catalogue, "James, Thomas", "James, Elinor"; McKenzie, ed., *Stationers' Company Apprentices 1641–1700*, 89, 101; McKenzie, ed., *Stationers' Company Apprentices 1701–1800*, 190–91; Nichols, *Literary Anecdotes*, 305–9, 334; Charles Welch, "James, Eleanor," in *The Dictionary of National Biography from the Earliest Times to 1900*, ed. Sir Leslie Stephen and Sir Sidney Lee (Oxford: Oxford University Press, 1921–22), 644–45. See also Paula McDowell, "James, Elinor," oxforddnb.com.

ବ Chapter Seven ଓ

Almanac Content

A close reading of the HRC sample offers an example of almanacs' utility as historical evidence and demonstrates the close parallels between the stationers' communal values and the thematic rhetoric of their products.

Almanacs and the Scientific Revolution

Considered from a modern perspective, the most foreign element of almanac content is astrology—the notion that the stars affect human events. Book almanacs varied from region to region, but many—particularly the English variety as it developed through the sixteenth and seventeenth centuries—were essentially astrological documents. Astrological practitioners in Elizabethan and Stuart England aggressively promulgated their craft through the genre until "almanac maker" became nearly (though not quite) synonymous with "astrologer." In his seminal work on the subject, Bernard Capp makes astrology the benchmark for judging the historical significance of the almanac genre; the more active and creative the astrology, the more important the almanac. In this view, eighteenth century almanacs represented a decline from the golden age of almanac making in the mid-1600s. If one accepts this standard, it is difficult to argue with Capp's view; the astrology in eighteenth century almanacs is stale, repetitive, bland, and parasitic. It plagiarized heavily from earlier astrological work and contributed nothing new to the art. Judged in this way, almanacs apparently offer strong evidence for a rapid and decisive shift from an irrational, archaic worldview to a rational, modern outlook. In short, they seem to affirm the traditional account of the scientific revolution and the emergence of modernity. Yet one can interpret almanacs to confirm a different view of early modern science, one which describes historical actors in their own terms rather than contemporary ones. Viewed from the latter position, almanacs offer a glimpse of the cosmology by which the people of early modern England understood their world, and their concerns become more intelligible.

Two Views

The traditional account of the scientific revolution tells "the appealing story of technical and conceptual innovation."[1] It is a Whiggish history, part of the rhetoric of enlightenment which has saturated our own culture with a reflexive belief in human development. Proponents of this view present a pantheon of intellectual pioneers—Copernicus, Brahe, Kepler, Descartes, Galileo, Bacon, Harvey, Boyle, Newton, etc.— who debunked the prevailing ignorance of older times with the insight of pure reason. Their courageous efforts, often in the face of persecution by their ignorant contemporaries, freed mankind from the shackles of superstition and allowed humans to take control of their destiny. It is a dramatic story, and a plausible one because it describes some obvious historical facts: we do think differently from our ancestors, and we can make and do and know things of which they did not even dream. This account's fundamental appeal lies not just in the narcissism of self-congratulation or even the reassurance of self-justification but also in its neat explanation of historical change. By reducing human belief into two categories—subjective superstition and objective knowledge—the present world becomes the inevitable outcome of a struggle between truth and falsehood. Human beings, it says, developed two basic hypotheses of the world: the old one is superstitious and the new one is rational. As the old ways of thinking were tested, their inadequacy relative to the new way became obvious. The old was discarded and the new embraced. In this view historical change is logical, with all of the inevitability—perhaps even predictability—of logic.[2]

The problem with the traditional account is that while it accounts for the present admirably well, it has trouble with the past. Busily dividing history up into heroes and villains—the relevant and irrelevant— it unconsciously assumes "that their thought patterns were fundamentally just like ours."[3] It presumes that "science" as we conceive of it must be essential and indivisible, existing (like a deity) whole and undefiled through all times and in all places. Historians taking this view unconsciously ignore large discrepancies between their story and the actual evidence left by their heroes. Although we find superstition and science continually mingled in hero and villain alike, we have no way to account for it. For example, when we find the heroic Isaac Newton practicing alchemy and speculating on theology with the same vigor that he pursued calculus and mechanics, we have no choice but to chalk it up to the eccentricity of genius—or perhaps schizophrenia. But surely this is historical solipsism. Recognizing this problem, we are faced with a choice: to either continue a resort to dubious platitudes or to admit that historical change may be so complex that it is ultimately beyond explanation. If the second possibility is true (and I think it is) then while we can see by comparison that change has occurred, we may lack the resources to account for it.[4]

This has all sorts of inconvenient implications. If reason, however pure, is inadequate for final explanations, we may never reach the Holy Grail of total certainty. Old may not be inherently worse than new after all, an admission that puts us in the tedious position of having to sift through old superstitions for truth and new truths for superstition. Phenomena may exist beyond the reach of our measurements. Our picture of things may be neither flawless nor destined for flawlessness; we may have to accept the unexpected and unpredictable, description instead of explanation, and hints rather than full disclosure. Yet messy and humiliating as the second option may be, it is surely the most likely choice. It has that ironic twist which daily experience leads us to expect of reality. It also allows historians to take the past seriously on its own terms, and to treat past generations as peers rather than intellectual toys.[5]

The Early Eighteenth Century Cosmos

If one takes this messier approach, one finds it odd but not laughable that almanac consumers in 1712 believed that the stars influenced their daily lives. As demonstrated earlier, the Company's almanac authorship was constrained largely by the market; they printed what would sell. Taken together, one could reasonably expect their almanacs to have reflected the spectrum of possible belief within early eighteenth century cosmology. It is significant, then, that the Company saw fit to dedicate considerable space to astrological themes in ten of the eighteen almanacs in the HRC sample.[6] This indicates that early eighteenth century thought took place within the bounds of "natural astrology": the idea that the stars (like the sun and moon) influenced natural conditions on earth, including the weather and disease. The primary cosmological debate portrayed in the almanacs involves the extent, not the existence, of the stars' power. Seven almanacs espoused "judicial," or predictive, astrology—arguing that the stars' influence was pervasive and governed by mathematical rules which made their effects predictable. Three almanacs portrayed a strictly natural position which held that the effects of astral power were unpredictable and of unknown extent. In the end, the most significant fact is that debate over astrology remained utterly unremarkable in early eighteenth century England.

Almanacs containing judicial astrology included *Astrologus Britannicus*, *Calendarium Astrologicum*, *Great News from the Stars*, *Merlinus Anglicanus*, *Perkins*, *Olympia Domata*, and *Vox Stellarum*. Regardless of the particular mathematical scheme that an almanac advocated, its actual predictions differed very little from all the others; the prophecies were universally bland. Where *Merlinus Anglicanus* prophesied, "Many weighty considerations in Hand this Quarter, and I hope all for the Best"; *Great News from the Stars* spoke of "several Matters and Things there, are now in somewhat an uncertain and uneasie Posture"; and *Speculum Uranicum* predicted "some Contest about Religion, and some one of the Long Robe meets with a frown from his Prince." One might be tempted to attribute such a tentative spirit to caginess, the suspicion that astrologers knew they were making bogus statements and so hedged their bets by formulations that meant nothing specific and could encompass a variety of situations. As demonstrated below, some antijudicial skeptics took precisely this view. From this perspective, the prophetic almanacs' failure to respond to antijudicial skeptics would seem suspicious. Yet one can also explain the judicial astrologers' refusal to heed their detractors and make more specific predictions in terms acceptable to their own system. From the judicial perspective, the skeptics' comments would have indicated gross ignorance of the prophetic craft. Their predictions were not based on inspiration like Old Testament prophets or intuitive insight like Greek oracles. Rather, judicial astrologists dealt in mathematically derived probabilities. The stars altered the physical world, and the human imagination was not exempt. Stars inclined people to act in a certain manner. Men could choose to overrule the stars, but the majority usually did not. Judicial astrology, like insurance actuarial tables, assumed that once they had accounted for the relevant variables "predictions about the behavior of large masses of men will often be verified."[7]

Three titles—*Apollo Anglicanus*, *Culpepper Revived*, and *Poor Robin*—contained vigorous attacks on the judicial position. Yet their arguments also marked out the limits of disagreement on this subject, indicating a general consensus on natural astrology that had nothing to do with the accuracy of predictions. In the most entertaining almanac for

1712, *Poor Robin* mocked judicial astrology with the same hyperactive parody it applied to every convention of the almanac genre. It made light of astrologers' penchant for generalized weather prediction. January, for instance, would have "Very bad Hay Weather," while February would surely be "a forward Spring of Rogues, Whores, Highway-men and Cut-purses." The ominously vague predictions that astrologers typically put in their calendars became social satire in *Poor Robin*: "Your vapouring Gallants shall swagger it out with gilded Rapiers by their sides; but to what purpose they wear those killing Ones, no body knows, unless to frighten fools, bully with Cowards, or draw on Link-Boys." Like Jonathan Swift's Bickerstaff, *Poor Robin* also offered an elaborate spoof prognostication, "an Ass-trological Scheme or Jimcrack, with Astrological Predictions, Prognostications and Observations upon it." And here, it offered a more sober case against judicial astrology:

> Take notice that I do not intend to hunt among the Stars for Prophecies, and News for future Ages, as if the Firmament were but a great Volume, or vast Sheet of Paper, and the Stars an Alphabet, in such manner disposed, as if God Almighty had written therein the Destiny of Kings and Kingdoms for these Men to read through a Jacob's Staff. Those Night Philosophers that have an Intellect as dark as the Time they study in, and a Brain as cloudy as the foggy Region they look through; are still looking through Tubes and Opticks, as if those silly Instruments could assist moral Sight to see into future Ages, and discern Things as far distant as the end of Time: They are continually peeping in the Moon and Stars as if they were so many Looking-Glasses, that did represent every Action, Motion and Gesture of Man below; and those not only present and past, but future too. As I detest the Practices of these Impostors, so I shall impose no such Lies upon the World; for my Predictions shall appear infallible as theirs uncertain, and as impossible to be False, as 'tis that the Sun should run counter, Rivers slide back into their Spring and the Moon lose her Way. . . .

Significantly, *Poor Robin* made a rhetorical distinction between the self-evident "immutable nature of Things, and convincing Axioms" derived from natural philosophy and the equation of judicial astrology with the mysticism of "our English Cybel, Mother Shipton [and] . . . Gipsy-Prophets." What *Poor Robin* portrayed as "superstition" was a straightforward "Art" in *Astrologus Britannicus*.

Where *Poor Robin* relied heavily on parody, *Apollo Anglicanus* applied a more prosecutorial technique to judicial astrology. *Apollo Anglicanus* combined satire, logic, research, Copernican astronomy, and theological injunction to refute astrology's truth-claims. Just as *Poor Robin's* "Ass-trology" was a "Jimcrack," *Apollo Anglicanus* presented it as the "frightful relations of Lemures, Lares and Lamiae, of Hobgoblings, Fairies, &t." *Apollo Anglicanus* confidently asserted that the majority of Englishmen had rejected astral prophecy, "[it] being in these Parts almost laugh'd and hiss'd off the Stage, and remaining only in such Countries where Ignorance and Blind Superstition are too much prevalent." The "sonorous Nothings" of judicial systems "may raise Predictions, which to the Timorous and Credulous may be as frightful as the Stories of Hobgoblings to Children, yet to the more Judicious it will but give occasion to laugh at and deride, or at least to suspect the whole Art to be but meer Forgeries and Fancies." Astrological dictums—including those of the revered Ptolemy—could only be "the Dotages and Fictions of Brainsick Men." Yet *Apollo Anglicanus* did not content itself with mere ridicule. Demonstrating detailed knowledge of astrological literature in its arguments, it quoted prominent astrological authorities at length and reeled off a bewildering list of jargon-laden aphorisms before demonstrating their logical incoherence. "Schemes" of planetary "Houses," lunar "Nodes," and stellar "Hours and Days" were "all arbitrarious; 'tis at the pleasure of the Architect; build as they please, 'tis all with as good success." The zodiac could just as easily have had twenty signs as twelve. Indeed, notions of "Dignities and Debilities" of celestial bodies led to absurdities like attributing the heat of summer to the "Dog-star" that was ascendant both in hot July and cold February, or concluding that nighttime darkness must result from "tenebrificous or dark Stars, by whose influence Night is brought on, for that they do ray out Darkness and Obscurity upon the Earth, as the Sun does Light." The simplicity of Copernican astronomy made it much more logical to attribute summer to the "advantageous posture of the Sun, he having been long near the Tropick of Cancer, and nearby hath heated the Earth," and to think of diurnal darkness as "the absence of the Sun" rather than the presence of dark stars. Perhaps most importantly, reason and mathematics accorded with scripture while astrology contradicted the Old Testament injunction, "Learn not the way of the Heathen, and be not dismayed at the signs of the Heaven, for the Heathen are dismayed at them."[8] Astrology was an "an old relick of Heathenish Superstition and Idolatry," the arbitrary contrivance of "Heathens [who] allotted days to their Stellary Gods, and worshipped the Host of Heaven." The bottom line though, was that astrology simply did not work. The astrologers' most prominent and consistent predictions failed to materialize:

> One E——ck——ff [sic][9] can in one Year kill an Astrologer that believes his own Art, and has, as he calls it, some un-lucky Direction operating; when many of our modern As-trologers cannot in Twenty Years kill a French Tyrant, with all their ill Directions, Projections, Transits, &c. but are so bar-barous to be always wounding and killing, still keeping him in lingring misery, yet will not dispatch him.

Following this allusion to Jonathan Swift's ironic *Bickerstaff Papers*, *Apollo Anglicanus* dedicated three very serious pages to cataloguing three decades' worth of explicit—and manifestly unfulfilled—predictions from three separate almanacs that Louis XIV would die soon.[10] The key point in this, historically speaking, was that *Apollo Anglicanus* did not debate the stars' influence on terrestrial conditions, only the utility of predictive systems. The difference lay in degree, not in kind.

If *Poor Robin* and *Apollo Anglicanus* represent an extreme anti-judicial position, *Culpepper Revived* held a centrist position. It rounded out its information on tides and fairs with an essay, "A Plain and Intelligible Description, of the Visible World," in which it examined the implications of Copernican astronomy. The "Geometrical Demonstrations" of Coper-nican theory had demonstrated the "exceeding Falsity" of Ptolemy's "hy-pothesis, and Theory of the Planetary Motions." In its place, Copernican astronomer-mathematicians had constructed a sophisticated model of planetary motion, distances, light sources, reflection, and positional rela-tivity which *Culpepper Revived* described in some detail.[11] This mechan-ical explanation for celestial light and motion offered such a reliable al-ternative to the personified heavens of Ptolemaic philosophy that a convinced reader could no longer believe in dark stars, seasonal stars, or the schemes of houses and dignities posited by astrology. Yet, *Culpep-per Revived* carefully delineated between the "Visible World" and the in-visible world, and rendered the first with confidence while withholding judgment on the latter. Copernicans had explained much about the uni-verse that had previously mystified mankind, but they had not explained it all. If the universe were mechanical and material, that did not mean that it was also devoid of mystery. Indeed, "we may reasonably conclude, that the Secret rays and Influence of these Coelestial Bodies, exert their Power and Force upon Men and all sublunary Things, more than Humane Rea-son can yet comprehend or know."[12] While it celebrated the evident precision of Copernican science, then, *Culpepper Revived* left room for atomic theory and quantum mechanics.

This element of uncertainty in *Culpepper Revived* highlighted the broad cosmological consensus shared by judicial practitioner and skeptic alike. Regardless of an almanac's position on astrology, its calendar inevitably included monthly weather predictions and listed a different body part for each day of the year.[13] Also, a significant minority of almanacs included articles on husbandry, gardening, and health. The content of these articles and the rationale behind annual weather predictions and body parts becomes clear when presented in light essays on mathematics and popular science presented by a few of the almanac writers.

The listing of a daily body part strikes a modern reader as the most odd. Often calendars were accompanied by a short description of the theory of the lunar anatomy—or as *Rose* put it, "The Moon's Dominion in Man's Body," which explains much about this practice. The theory of lunar anatomy held that as the moon passed into "conjunction" with various zodiacal constellations, it exerted a special influence on various parts of the human body. Depending on the scheme, a certain orientation of moon and zodiac might make the beginning of a month auspicious for setting arm bones, while as the orientations changed, the middle of a month might be appropriate for purging bowels. If an Englishman who held to this theory had an ache in his neck on the ninth of April or twisted his ankle on the eighteenth or felt especially clear-headed on the twenty-seventh, he could explain this in terms of the moon's influence, just as he explained ocean tides. The moon's influence might have been helpful or harmful, but either way, it was undoubtedly strong.

Quite often, explanatory articles centered on the Man of Signs, a woodcut engraving that featured a hermaphroditic nude with female breasts and male genitals seated on a globe and surrounded by the zodiac. Lines pointed out the various combinations of celestial bodies with human anatomy. Eleven of the eighteen almanacs in this sample included such an explanatory article, and nearly all of them listed body parts alongside sunrise and saints' days on their calendars. Some Englishmen clearly doubted the reliability of lunar medical theory, but whether or not this particular relationship between moon and body part was valid, the notion that celestial bodies affected the physical condition on the surface of the earth appeared axiomatic. The theory of lunar anatomy may or may not have been a misapplication of a valid principle, but either way, the principle held.

Utility and truth appear to have been the least of the Company's priorities when it came to the Man of Signs. The little naked figure was perhaps more emblematic of the genre than the dead authors, and the Company required its inclusion on purely commercial grounds. The

Man of Signs was obligatory because, as the *Great Britain's Diary* explained,

> Should I omit to place this Figure here,
> My Book would hardly sell another Year:
> What (quoth my Country Friend) D'ye think I'll buy
> An Almanack without th' Anatomy?
> As for its Use, nor he, nor I can tell;
> However, since it pleases all so well,
> I've put it in, because my Book shou'd sell.

Poor Richard mocked him with doggerel:

> Here I sit naked, like some Fairy Elf,
> My Seat a Pumpkin; I grudge no Man's Pelf;
> Though I've no Bread nor Chees upon my Shelf;
> I'll tell the gratis, when it safe is,
> To purge, to bleed, or cut, thy Cattle, or—thy self.[14]

But whether in Philadelphia or in London, good business sense in the eighteenth century kept the Man of Signs on his throne.

Understanding this bit of astral medicine helps make sense of the almanacs' annual meteorological forecasts. Like the near-universal listing of daily body parts, almost every almanac calendar included monthly weather predictions, and—as with the Man of Signs—this practice bore little if any relationship to a given almanac's stance on prophecy. Natural astrology meant that by calculating the positions of the heavenly bodies, one could gauge the probable influence of those configurations on the earth. Whatever their take on judicial astrology, most readers evidently considered it reasonable to predict the weather, at least in general terms, over a year ahead of time. Or perhaps this too was at least partly a commercial convention.

The same system that made it reasonable to predict the weather twelve months in advance also allowed almanacs to give highly specific advice on the timing of household and farming tasks based on purely mathematical calculations. Typical of these, *Calendarium Astrologicum* advised husbandmen to

> Kill fat Swine near the Full and their Fat shall hold boyling better, and longer, than that killed at other times.
>
> Gather Apples and other Fruits, Herbs and Flowers to have them large and fair, the Moon increasing, and towards the Full; Gather them in a dry season, the Moon Increasing, in good aspect of Jupiter or Venus, so they will keep well.

Together with the lunar anatomy and annual meteorology such husbandry advice completed a pattern. Whatever an Englishman living in
this milieu may have thought of one or the other of these theories, and
whatever his belief may have been about prognostication, he accepted
as axiomatic the direct physical interaction of celestial and terrestrial
entities. He conceived of no such thing as "outer space." In 1712, all
space was unitary, or at least organically integrated.

Several essays on science and math contained in both pro- and
anti-prophecy almanacs delineated this concept of the cosmos. The
heavily astrological *Speculum Uranicum* included an essay on the "physical Reasons of the Portents of the Blazing-stars or Comets," which indicated a great deal about the current theory of the physical universe:

And first it is very apparent [comets] are the Caus of inordi-
nate Heat, by their ardent burning in the Air, and their Matter of which they are composed, and the Earth left dry, and so
the Moisture by which it fructified all Things growing therein
is dry'd up by excessive Heat, and so render'd barren; whence
there must of necessity follow Famine, &c. in those nations
or Kingdoms where they are seen, or from whence their Substance was drawn.

The Air is by them also infected through hot, thick Ex-
halations, which being drawn into the Mouths of Living Creatures does infect and kill them, causing Pestilential Diseases;
also by their excessive Heat, the Radical Moisture of Living
Creatures (whereby they subsist) is dry'd up, whereby they
become little better than dead Carcasses; therefore it is good,
in such Times, to use cool and moistening Things which are
of a restorative Nature.

Again, When a Comet does appear there are many Ex-
halations in the Air, and those of nature hot and dry; which
dry up the Humours in men and increase Choler, which ex-
cites to Quarrels, then follow Blows, Wars and Bloodshed; and
so by Consequence produces Alterations in States, Law, governments, &c. in those Places that behold 'em, &c. Comets
also cause Winds, and Winds trouble the Sea, whence come
Inundations and overflowing of Rivers. Thus, though I have
delivered the Reasons of the Portents of Comets, I would not
have any one to fear, tho' they be never so horrid or terrible to
behold, but rather take Courage thereby to cal earnestly upon
God for Mercy, that he may avert his Judgments, whereof he
does fairly warn us by these his Messengers, &c.

Intelligent people feared comets for purely material reasons. Given that comets were dry and hot, and given that they passed through the same "Substance" that surrounded the creatures of the earth who need moisture to thrive, one suspects that even *Poor Richard* held comets responsible for harmful effects. Lacking evidence of a vacuum in outer space, *Speculum Uranicum* quite reasonably assumed that the stars, planets, sun, moon, and comets were all suspended in a substance contiguous with the air on earth. It followed that comets were viewed as natural disasters on a par with tsunamis, tornadoes, and earthquakes. If the effects of a comet were less direct and immediate than a tidal wave, the image of wheat shriveling in the field as a comet passed overhead remained a vivid one indeed. A comet passing through a contiguous atmosphere would generate turbulence like a boat on a pond whose waves would, of course, travel through the integrated cosmos and wash over the planet earth.

The thoroughgoing anti-prophet *Apollo Anglicanus* conveyed the same basic view of the universe as his astrologist opponents. The almanac explained that

> It cannot be denied but that the Planets and fixed Stars, but more especially the sun and Moon, have influence upon; and hereby some modest conjectures may be made of the constitution and change of the Air, and alteration of the Weather, so far as it ariseth from these first Qualities, and is collected from long Observation and Experience, and not from the odd and whimsical Rules of ancient Writers, who lived in remote and very different Climates from ours; though this may and ought to be allowed, yet the other secret influence dreamed of, and pretended to be discovered by Astrologers, viz. such as pretend to the Resolving Horary Questions, calculating of Nativities, giving account of mundane Affairs, such as the rising and fall of Great Men, Nations, and Kingdoms; and also teach the Doctrine of Elections for the beginning of any work, seems much to be questioned; for though it be allowed, as aforesaid, that the Sun, and other Caelestial Bodies, do cause in the Terrestrial, heat, cold, dryness and moisture, doth it therefore follow that these Effects do declare before-hand the constitution of Mens bodies, the disposition of mens minds, the affection of mens hearts, or what success they shall have in their various affairs, touching Health, Wealth, Honour and Religion? But in order to know these things, the learned Astrologer having many plausible pretences, hath recourse to his Astrological Rules. . . .

Both advocates and skeptics of judicial astrology worked from the same "plausible pretences." Both accepted the same basic model of the cosmos even if they chose to attribute different levels of significance to it.

This evidence from a single annual cycle of the Company's almanacs offers a snapshot of the mindset that prevailed among people living in early eighteenth century England. Like any snapshot, the limited perspective of this picture probably distorts it to some extent, but the image we get is nonetheless coherent. The cosmology of early eighteenth century almanacs would have been largely familiar to medieval, even ancient thinkers, and it is profoundly foreign to us. Yet the emphasis of various elements differed slightly from the medieval or Renaissance worldview. The almanacs reflected the contemporary discourse described in Patrick Curry's *Prophecy and Power*:

> In the sixteenth and seventeenth centuries, the line supposedly dividing natural from judicial astrology became heavily policed . . . both sides more than ever divided, became committed to an interminable struggle to push the boundary in one direction or another—a contest neither side could win outright. . . . Both the boundary and the struggle, of course, were predicated on the reality of astrological influences as such.

What the almanacs do not convey is any sense that the premises of natural astrology had become "increasingly problematic," or that "a new intellectual universe" was developing. One may find such a sense in other sources, but to understand early eighteenth century England is to accept a world in which most people literally cohabited with the stars. It was a world that took for granted "a sense of connectedness with the cosmos."[15] Such an understanding did not preclude the importance of calculus and physics; it saw no conflict at all between such fields of knowledge and astrology. Holding a perfectly plausible position in his world, a practicing judicial astrologer such as John Wing would naturally admire "the incomparable Sir Isaac Newton" for his scientific contributions, and approve of mathematics because it "adds a manly vigour to the mind, and frees it from Prejudice, Credulity, and Superstition . . . by accustoming us to examin and not to take things upon trust . . . [and freeing] us from those mean and narrow thoughts which Ignorance and Superstition are apt to beget in us." Wing could deride superstition and embrace prophetic astrology in the same breath because the early eighteenth century concept of the world made astrology plausible. If ideas today differ in substance, the contemporary situation historically remains much the same.

Indeed, the project of examining old almanacs tends to reduce the temptation to privilege the present generation's worldview over those of dead and unborn counterparts. After being confronted by the knowledge of a former time, current understandings are instantly situated within the historical process. It helps one to recognize that any of today's self-evident assumptions may well become the next generation's absurdity. It also reminds that one can have no better idea what will seem rational two centuries from now than John Wing did two centuries ago. There are no logical limitations to the historical development of knowledge, no teleological boundaries to the process. Judicial astrology is unthinkable today, but perhaps for that very reason there are no assurances that something very much like it will not become self-evident tomorrow. If history has lessons, perhaps its first lesson is humility, and its corollary is a sort of inter-epochal golden rule: judge the past if you must, but only as you would wish to be judged by the future. One might call it chronological courtesy.

Politics and Mathematicks: The Supreme Virtue of Order

Almanacs had their brightest moment in the historiographic sun when Linda Colley published her influential study of British nationalism, *Britons: Forging the Nation 1707–1837*. She included almanacs to demonstrate the wide extent of a fundamentally Protestant identity, defined against a Catholic Other. Curiously, she further highlighted almanacs with a picture of the frontispiece of *The Protestant Almanac* published in 1700, seven years before the legal birth of the British nation that was her subject. One finds it significant in this regard that *The Protestant Almanac* was published from 1668 to 1700, which made Colley's copy the final edition of the entire series.[16] That particular almanac marked the decline of a trend more characteristic of Restoration England than Hanoverian Britain. A look at the HRC almanacs shows that, while Francophobia and anti-Catholicism remained, other themes had gained equal prominence by the early eighteenth century.

Ten of those almanacs—over half—included significant political commentary of some sort. The Pope, Rome, and France figure rather less prominently, however, than one might expect after reading *Britons*. Another theme runs through all of the political talk at least as consistently as hatred of Catholicism or France, and this poses difficulties for a scheme such as Colley's. Many of these political references were concerned with the benefits of unity and portrayed an intense fear that the domestic status quo might be disrupted by civil strife. They presented the interests of individual subjects as linked inextricably with the fate of the current regime. The dominant theme was a simple desire for national unity and a straightforward fear of strife. Perhaps especially because of John Partridge's temporary absence, this theme lacked partisan flavor—conveying a sense of disgust with factional divisions of every sort.

Where they explicitly addressed questions of national identity, the Company's almanacs focused not on the essential difference between Colley's Britons and her Catholic Other but on the different personal status enjoyed by English and French subjects. *Angelus Britannicus* included a poem above its calendar, and the August stanza presented the French as fellow humans—possibly even cousins—with a potential for liberty equal to any Englishman.

> Could France but once her Liberty regain,
> Refame her Liberty, shake off her Chain;
> She'd never more become a Passive land,
> Or seek another Lewis to Command:
> Sure this may let a Neighbouring nation see,
> How they despise their own Felicity.

In a similar vein, the September stanza presented the "Ruine" of the French people as a tragedy among kinfolk rather than the demise of an enemy.

> 'Tis strange indeed that France so long forbears
> To use all other Arms but Prayers and Tears;
> 'Tis strange that France should so long patient prove.
> And bear the burthen, which she might remove,
> For Britains, if their King's a Tyrant grown,
> Resist and pull their Sacred Monarch down.
> but yet no Motives will successful prove,
> Nor the most urgent Reason Britains move;
> Though they the folly of their wishes view,
> Those very former wishes they pursue;
> And tho' their Ruine's plain before their face,
> Their Ruine they with open arms embrace.

Frenchmen represented not categorical opposites, but corrupted brethren whose fate could easily befall unwary Britons. Conversely, the French merited English-style liberty even if they mysteriously chose not to grasp it. This lends support to Colin Kidd's thesis that early modern identities depended not on binary contrasts but on "degrees of consanguinity among a world of nations descended from Noah."[17] Such evidence also serves as a caution against reductionist theories in the writing of history.

In more general terms, the almanacs pressed home a common theme of stability and satisfaction with the status quo. *Angelus Britannicus*'s calendar poem was typical in this regard. It returned continually to the theme of unity, happiness, and peace. The stanza for January equated "Union" with "Peace" and happiness, and contrasted these with "Discord," "Feuds," and "Disobedience":

> When will Unhappy Britain grow more Wise?
> For want of Wisdom Happiness denies.
> Will Britain ever more to Union come?
> And gain a Peace abroad, by Peace at home.
> Or will Eternal Discord still appear?
> And Feuds return with each returning Year?
> Long our late Glorious Monarch strove to show
> We might be Happy, nay, he taught us how;
> Bid us unite, for Universal Peace
> must cause an Universal happiness
> But not his Wishes, nor more just Command,
> Could move a Stubborn Disobedient Land.

The February stanzas indicated the hand of evil conspiracy—French Catholicism embodied in the Jacobite Pretender—behind any "Discord . . . Broils . . . Parties . . . Rage . . . [or] Feuds." The problem with France, Catholicism, and the Pretender, however, was not so much their religious or ethnic difference as the threat they posed to civil harmony as such.

> How grat must be the Folly of Mankind,
> When Nations are to Discord thus inclin'd?
> 'Tis strange how small a Thing will Broils excite,
> But st [sic] anger still that Men in Broils delight:
> For such there are who into Parties fly,
> Rage at they know not what, they know not why
> But is it Pleasure that they thus pursue?
> Or have these Men some other Ends in view?
> Thus only we the Riddle can explain;
> Thus shows why Parties, why these Feuds remain;
> by shewing there's an Hand behind the Scene,
> Which moves with dextrous Art the whole Machine.

April's verse was clearly anti-Catholic, alleging that the "Seats of Learning" were the unwitting dupes of "the Jesuit's Scheme." The primary fear involved, however, was not that scholars might subscribe to transubstantiation. Rather, the danger lay in the potential "ruin" brought on by

"Difference" between British subjects. Again domestic harmony was the objective, and unity was the means to that end. Unity meant security; division meant trouble; and the "Jesuits" meant division.

> How e'en our Seats of Learning guilty prove,
> Which we may well suppose their Country love;
> Why these, or most of these, tho' Wise they seem,
> Unthinking carry on the Jesuits Scheme;
> If not, altho' they han't the Jesuits Name,
> The Mask but once thrown off they're much the same
> Thus far we see the Vulgar are deceiv'd
> And Crafty Rogues can make themselves believ'd;
> but then you'll ask, how come our Men of Sense
> To show such Folly by their Difference?
> How these are guilty, tho' their Country's Friends
> Of that, which to its certain ruin tends.

As with April, May's verse considered the evil of "Rome" and "Romish Priests" to be axiomatic. Yet here again the fear was not theological but instead social and political—"Party-Fury . . . The Nation's Epidemical Disease" which results in counterproductive "Feuds."

> Whence came the Churches Danger but from Rome?
> From whence its real Ruin yet may come:
> If they no only who her Members are,
> But even those who her Revenues share;
> Those very notions, and those Doctrines use,
> Which Romish Priests would have us introduce.
> But since the Cause is plain, why Feuds arise,
> I now must humbly offer my Advice;
> And beg you'll let all Party-Fury cease,
> The Nation's Epidemical Disease:
> And if you'd any dubious Points decide,
> Let Argument and Reason be your Guide.

October's verse condemned "Quarrels . . . Division . . . Contention . . . [and] Domestic Jars" as "more dangerous . . . than forreign wars."

> Forbear at length, no more absurdly Act
> No more condemn the crimes which ye protect;
> No more let Quarrels about that appear,
> Which whether just or not, you need not fear:
> While Sacred ANN o're these our Realms presides,
> And Britain's Queen for Britain's Health presides.

> Let all Division, all Contention cease,
> This be your only Strife, your QUEEN to please;
> Compose your many old Domestic Jars,
> Which are more dangerous far than foreign wars:
> Fro those wou'd quickly have their wish'd for end,
> If these did not our Enemies defend.

The November stanza related the principle of unity to the War of the Spanish Succession. *Angelus Britannicus* was preoccupied not with an Other but with preserving "Union" by avoiding "Jars" and "Party."

> Tho' Marlborough their Towns and Cities Storms,
> And in the Field his mighty Acts performs;
> Tho' daily he his Conquests shall extend,
> But we in daily Jars at Home contend;
> Not all his mighty Conquests yes will do,
> 'Tis Union alone must strike the Blow.
> Could this this [sic] be to its full perfection brought,
> And once the Name of Party be forgot;
> Tho Haughty Monarch, who hath long with ease,
> Distrub'd not only ours, but Europe's Peace;
> Would be for our Victorious Arms too weak,
> And soon at ANNA's Throne Protection seek.

The rhetoric in *Angelus Britannicus* evinced an unmistakable sense of weariness with the tumultuous party politics that marked Anne's reign. While Capp correctly observes that some late Stuart almanacs participated vigorously in the contests of the day, this was not the whole picture. Many of the Company's customers evidently disliked all parties equally.

Other almanacs included similar themes. In its prognostication section *Astrologus Britannicus* betrayed an obsession with civil strife similar to that in *Angelus Britannicus*. "The Papists" would be "ploting and cabaling against the Governments the[y] live under" in April, but they were not the only source of trouble. English Protestants were also to blame, being "apt to envy and disturb each other, according to their different Interests and Perswasions, provoking each other with discriminating epithets, and opprobrious Notes of Distinction." December's wish was simply for protection from "designing Enemies" and that "the British Throne may never want such a Protestant Successor as is now by Law Established." In a short poem beneath its regal table, *Calendarium Astrologicum* worried about Jacobitism and the Pretender—"Treation . . . [and a] Proud Traitor"—and wished Queen Anne Godspeed in the effort to "quell proud Rebels." *Culpepper Revived* affirmed simply that "The Constitution of our Laws are good" in its table of judicial terms. If anything, these phrases complemented the thematic paranoia in *Angelus Britannicus* and *Astrologus Britannicus* that "designing Enemies" might snatch away potential blessings of the standing order.

Similarly, *Merlinus Anglicanus* observed in its prognostications that

> Societies are preserved by Mutual Benefits wisely interchanged, therefore let none Foolishly strive to break that Sacred Tye; Let each Man quietly and contentedly discharge the proper Duties of his Station, and then all will Thrive and Prosper, but Envy and Dissention, destroys the best of Constitutions.

The concern here was clearly preserving prosperity, and prosperity was predicated on the "Sacred Tye" of domestic unity. The immediate threat to the average subject's well-being was discontent, disquiet, usurpation, and "Envy and Dissention." The passage continued this theme in a paean to unity:

> When the Superior members of a State,
> Refuse their Tribute to the Magistrate;
> And will the Nobles Level, soon they come,
> Involv'd together to the Fatal Tomb.
> By civil Broils the Mob destroy their Kings,
> And that one general Devastation brings.
> When each with mutual Ardour strive to Love,
> The whole with Order does, and Beauty move,
> But when Convulsions and Dissentions rend,
> 'Tis Plain that shatter'd State, will quickly end.

The legacy of the English Civil War echoed plainly here—mobs destroying the reigns of kings, and nobles refusing to give deference to the monarch. *Merlinus Anglicanus* portrayed the terrifying prospect of a repeat. Nothing could have been worse than the "Fatal Tomb [of a] shatter'd State," not even, presumably, having a Hanoverian on the throne instead of a Stuart. The immediate threat of "Convulsions and Dissentions" loomed heavy in this almanac (as it did in *Astrologus Britannicus* and *Angelus Britannicus*), equaled only by the hope for "Order . . . and Beauty." The world as painted in *Merlinus Anglicanus* was a place where

> Many set their Wits on Work, Struggle and Strive for the upper Hand, never heeding who falls, so they get up; and notwithstanding they see so many go daily to the Grave, before their Eyes, Live as tho' they should never Dye; taking care for this

Earthly mammon which will Perish, like themselves, and never think of the Bread of Life, which will never Perish or Decay . . . let us all Unite and Pray.

Long Live Great Anne, our Gracious Sovereign,
Let none Resist, but all Her Right maintain;
Against the Gallic Tyrant let's advance,
And make a Peace within the Heart of France;
Lets lay by Canting of a Proud Pretender,
But Pray God still Defend, our Faith Defender.

Nothing was more important than life and peace. Peace, of course, meant the rule of a benevolent sovereign. The French, far from being monsters in essence, would have enjoyed the same benefits had they not been victimized by their tyrant king.

Continuing the theme, *Vox Stellarum*'s calendar poem emphasized the new national union in phrases such as "the *British* Throne" and "Brave Britain." It celebrated the Act of Union as a source of peace and stability:

Justice does now the Royal Scepter hold,
And those reliev'd that were to Ruin fold,
No Foreign Foe e'er shall our Borders vex,
Nor yet Domestick ones our Minds perplex
England to Monarchy is always bent.
Pray God preserve the Queen and Parliament.

France was a problem, but the danger was close to home too. *Vox Stellarum* decried

Rebel Man, perverse in every thing,
No Fear to God, nor Honour for the King!

It mentioned "Traytors" who incur "the People's Hate . . . Those that our Constitution would destroy," and "those that seek [the Queen's and Church's] Ruin." Its astrological predictions spoke of "a dissatisfy'd People, who cannot, nay will not, be contented to live quiet under the best Government in the World" and "some that cry out against Popery, and, at the same time, are doing the Pope's Business [by disrupting civil life]." Like *Merlinus Anglicanus*, *Vox Stellarum* concluded that

Broils and intestine Jars prove fatal not only to Families but to whole Nations; when Union and perfect Love is the Strength, the Glory, and Preservation of both. Thus you see this great Fabrick, the World could not stand except it be upheld by Union, which is the Bond of Peace and Love.

Yet again, "Broils and intestine Jars" held a prominent place next to anti-French canards. The almost frantic argument for "Union" echoed the sentiments contained in other almanacs.

Olympia Domata and *Great Britain's Diary: or, The Union-Almanack* reflected the general obsession with political unity, and they connected this political theme with another eighteenth century pre-occupation: mathematics.

Great Britain's Diary: or, The Union-Almanack, as its title suggests, used the British union of 1707 as a thematic device. It characterized political union as a universal imperative for all societies desiring happiness and security. The work began with an Aesopian fable entitled "No Security without UNITY." The tale described a man teaching his sons to cooperate for their mutual benefit by contrasting a single arrow, which they easily snapped into pieces, with a bundle of arrows, which none of them could break. The moral was clear:

> Collective Bodies in Close Union join'd,
> Remain invincible when so combin'd;
> But when divided are an easy Prey:
> The whole does in its weaken'd Parts decay.
> So a compacted Wall is firm and strong,
> Maintains its Ground, and braves Time's Fury long:
> But when one Stone does from its Station fall,
> Encroaching Ruin quickly shatters all.

Like other almanacs, this one portrayed no middle ground between "Close Union" and "Encroaching Ruin." Its primary concern was contention, quarrels, and internal disputes. To drive the point home, "A Brief Account of the Chief Battels between the English and the Scots, since the Norman Conquest: And of the necessity of a UNION between the Two nations" followed Aesop. In a list of fights from the 1139 battle of Conton in Yorkshire to Muscleborough Field in 1547, Great Britain's Diary demonstrated that

> When England and Scotland were Two distinct Monarchies . . .
> did they worry and destroy each other, till they were happily
> UNITED in King James VIth. of Scotland, and Ist. of England.
> . . . But our Sovereign Queen ANNE being now the only sur-
> viving Branch of that Family, In case the Happy UNION of the
> Two Kingdoms had not been made, May 1. 1707. the Kingdom
> of Scotland, after Her Decease, would have been at Liberty to
> have chose themselves a King: And then in all likelihood, the
> ancient Animosities between the Two Nations would have been

> Revived, and the like dreadful Scenes of Blood and Horror,
> would in a short time be acted over again, to the infinite Detri-
> ment of both Kingdoms. But, Blessed be GOD that dismal
> Prospect is vanished by the UNION. . . . And tho' some may
> be uneasy at present, no doubt but Time and a serious Reflec-
> tion on the Necessity of it, will reconcile them to it. However,
> POSTERITY Her Pious care shall Bless,
> While Men love Freedom, and are pleas'd with PEACE.

"Divisions" from this perspective equated to death. The preeminent concern was to avoid more of the "dreadful Scenes of Blood and Horror"
that had characterized English, Scottish, and British experiences for
many centuries. The overriding sentiment was not animus toward a
Catholic Other or an opposing party, but rather an abiding weariness
with the discord and destruction of the past, an earnest hope for peace,
and an absolute conviction that unity was the key to a secure future. Notably, after numerous pages of practical information, the almanac ended
with a mathematics demonstration—including a multiplication table and
several pages of example problems.

Following a similar pattern, *Olympia Domata* presented a political
poem centering on unity.

> Strike home my Muse, the Storm is past and gone,
> And calmer Days no doubt are coming on:
> Some still are learning what they may repent,
> And what they will not tell, is there intent;
> 'Tis pity Friendship, Unity and Peace,
> Shou'd be abus'd, or e'er have cause to cease:
> If all cou'd study but each others good,
> Then would these tings be better understood:
> We all may wish it so with one accord,
> Then wou'd our Lives more happiness afford.
>
> Hence therefore if with us, all is not well,
> It must appear our Natures do Rebell:
> 'Tis haughtiness and Pride amongst the rest,
> Which makes bad worse, yet cannot stand the Test;
> But with consent let's leave these crooked ways,
> In Peace, Content and Love conclude our Days.

Olympia Domata followed the rest in equating "happiness" with
"Friendship, Unity and Peace . . . one accord . . . Content and Love." It
simply hoped for "calmer Days." The enemy was not the Pope or the

French but "the Storm" of conflict and the crooked path of a rebellious nature.

This theme of order continued in a "Brief Discourse concerning the Excellency and Usefulness of Mathematical Learning." Math was important in part because of its "subservency to other Arts" and its "usefulness for the improvement of Commerce and Trade." It demonstrated the harmonious order of "the System of the World," "the Machine of the universe," and the orderly "rules of this Science."[18] Math offered everyone a sense of his position in the great scheme, "a true Idea of a place . . . to know the relation it hath to any other place, as to the distance and bearing, its Climate, Heat, cold, length of Days, &c." It added predictability and stability to every aspect of life; it "reduced Musick to a regular System, by contriving its Scales" which had the happy effect of preventing this "Art" from degenerating into a mere "Enthusiastick Rapture."

In both *Olympia Domata* and *Great Britain's Diary*, order in any sphere was intrinsically desirable. Political unity and mathematical calculations complimented one another because they were productive, sane and beneficial to common folk. The multiplication tables stood alongside a vivid history of "Blood and Horror" for good reason. The destructive chaos of the past was made to feel all too near, and in contrast the benefits of a mathematically ordered civil life became self-evident.

While this incessant theme of order and stability tends to complicate her monolithic Catholic Other thesis, it supports another of Colley's observations. She attributes the failure of the Jacobite rebellions to the same desire for order conveyed in these almanacs. She considers widespread yearning for stability to be the most logical explanation for the "seething passivity" that characterized the popular British response to Jacobitism and Jacobite invasions. A Jacobite coup

> Was almost certain to lead to a considerable loss of British lives, a large-scale destruction of property, widespread disorder and the disruption of trade . . . The price of its victory would almost certainly have been prolonged civil war . . . to many of their opponents it was the Jacobites themselves who were the insidious agents of division, while the ruling dynasty was the best guarantee for a measure of quiet and abundance . . . fear of invasion and civil war certainly played a part in hardening opinion against the Stuart cause.[19]

One would be hard put to formulate a more perfect paraphrase of the Company's almanacs than this, particularly in the war-weary year of 1711. It is by no means self-evident that "Protestantism provided the positive, most fundamental reason for coming down in support of the existing order." On the contrary, in 1711 at least, maintenance of the existing order seems to have provided the most fundamental reason for coming down in support of Protestantism.

One may reasonably view this sentiment as typical of the era. With the post-Revolution monarchy more or less firmly established, Britons had leisure to reflect on the bloody, chaotic century behind them. Perhaps a great many of them decided that, while political ideals and religious principles had their place, prosperity and harmony were worth a great deal more in practical terms.[20] Perhaps it became increasingly difficult to figure a price for one's own skin. Survival and social stability remain the most under-rated motives in historical analysis. The Stationers' Company, on the other hand, under-rated them not at all.

Notes

1. Charles Webster, *From Paracelsus to Newton: Magic and the Making of Modern Science* (Cambridge University, Cambridge, 1980).

2. Classic accounts from this traditional perspective include Herbert Butterfield, *The Origins of Modern Science, 1300–1800*, rev. ed. (New York: Free Press, 1957) 1; Bernard Cohen, *The Revolution in Science* (Cambridge, MA: Harvard University Press, 1985); Richard S. Westfall, *The Construction of Modern Science: Mechanisms and Mechanics* (New York: John Wiley, 1971).

3. B. J. T. Dobbs, "Newton as Final Cause and First Mover," in *Rethinking the Scientific Revolution*, ed. Margaret J. Osler (Cambridge: Cambridge University Press, 2000), 34.

4. Useful introductions to the problems with the traditional account and to the historiography of revisionist accounts include I. Bernard Cohen, ed., *Puritanism and the Rise of Modern Science: The Merton Thesis* (New Brunswick, NJ: Rutgers University Press, 1990); Margaret J. Osler, ed., *Rethinking the Scientific Revolution* (Cambridge: Cambridge University Press, 2000). Revisionist histories run the gamut from those who seek nuanced accounts of the scientific revolution to those who border on denial of any discernable "revolution" at all. Charles Webster probably epitomizes the former approach while Betty Jo Teeter Dobbs tends toward the second extreme. A look at any of the following will pay intellectual dividends: Andrew Cunningham, *The Anatomical Renaissance: The Resurrection of the Anatomical Projects of the Ancients* (Brookfield, VT: Ashgate, 1997); Allen G. Debus, *The Chemical Philosophy: Paracelsian Science and Medicine in the Sixteenth and Seventeenth Centuries* (New York: Neale Watson, 1977); Betty Jo Teeter Dobbs, *The Foundations of*

Newton's Alchemy: or, "The Hunting of the Greene Lyon" (Cambridge: Cambridge University Press, 1975); B. J. T. Dobbs, *The Janus Face of Genius: The Role of Alchemy in Newton's Thought* (Cambridge: Cambridge University Press, 1991); James E. Force, "Newton's God of Dominion: The Unity of Newton's Theological, Scientific, and Political Thought," in *Essays on the Context, Nature, and Influence of Isaac Newton's Theology,* ed. Richard H. Popkin and Fore (Dordrecht: Kluwer, 1990); Robert G. Frank, Jr., *Harvey and the Oxford Physiologists: A Study in Scientific Ideas* (Berkeley: University of California Press, 1980); Amos Funkenstein, *Theology and the Scientific Imagination from the Middle Ages to the Seventeenth Century* (Princeton: Princeton University Press, 1986); Reijer Hooykaas, *Religion and the Rise of Modern Science* (Edinburgh: Scottish Academic Press, 1972); William R. Newman, "Boyle's Debt to Corpuscular Alchemy," in *Robert Boyle Reconsidered,* ed. Michael Hunter (Cambridge: Cambridge University Press, 1994), 91–116; Lawrence Principe, *The Aspiring Adept: Robert Boyle and His Alchemical Quest; Including Boyle's "Lost" Dialogue on the Transmutation of Metals* (Princeton: Princeton University Press, 1998); P. M. Rattansi and J. E. McGuire, "Newton and the 'Pipes of Pan,'" *Notes and Records of the Royal Society of London* 21, 2 (1966), 108–143; Paolo Rossi, *Francis Bacon: From Magic to Science,* trans. Sacha Rabinovitch (New York: Routledge, 1968); Charles Webster, *Samuel Hartlib and the Advancement of Learning* (Cambridge: Cambridge University Press, 1970); Charles Webster, *The Great Instauration: Science, Medicine, and Reform 1626–1670* (New York: Holmes and Meier, 1976); Charles Webster, "From Paracelsus to Newton: Magic and the Making of Modern Science"; Jan W. Wojcik, *Robert Boyle and the Limits of Reason* (Cambridge: Cambridge University Press, 1997); Frances Yates, *Giordano Bruno and the Hermetic Tradition* (New York: Vintage, 1964).

5. This is, of course, a clumsy swipe at "presentism" in historical writing. More complete statements by much better qualified scholars can be found in Sir Herbert Butterfield, *The Whig Interpretation of History* (G. Bell & Sons, London, 1930); Yehvoa Elkana, "Two-Tier Thinking: Philosophical Realism & Historical Relativism" *Social Studies of Science* 8, no. 3 (1978), 309–26. Adrian Wilson and Timothy Ashplant, "Whig History and Present-Centered History," *Historical Journal* 31, no. 1 (1988), 1–16.

6. The almanacs in this sample exhibited a broad range of content with certain near-universal conventions. Of eighteen titles, most contained information on solar and lunar rhythms (17), a monthly calendar (17), and a historical chronology (14). Many contained the "lunar anatomy" addressed later in this essay (11), a calendar of judicial terms (9), information on money exchange rates and interest calculations (9), tide tables (8), eclipse calculations (8), a regal table (8), and essays on astrology (8), or science and math (8). A few contained husbandry and health advice (7), a list of famous cities with their direction and distance from London (6), a list of fairs (6), a list of highways (6), advertisements (6), preformatted legal forms (4), and measurement tables (3).

7. Clive Staples Lewis, *The Discarded Image: An Introduction to Medieval and Renaissance Literature* (Cambridge: Cambridge University Press, 1964), 104. For an excellent summary of the technical nuances of early modern astrology, see Patrick Curry, *Prophecy and Power: Astrology in Early Modern England* (Princeton: Princeton University Press, 1989), 8–18. See also Ann Geneva, *Astrology and the Seventeenth Century Mind: William Lilly and the Language of the Stars* (New York: Manchester University Press, 1995).

8. *Apollo Anglicanus* was quoting Jeremiah 10:2.

9. Despite the original transcription error of "E" for "I", his is clearly a reference to Isaac Bickerstaff, Dean Swift's persona in the widely celebrated practical joke that he played on John Partridge in 1706–9. For a succinct and insightful account of this episode, see Curry, *Prophecy and Power*, 89–91.

10. See also Capp, *English Almanacs*, 258.

11. *Culpepper Revived* included "these Astronomical truths" in an orderly list:

1. We find that the Sun and Fixed Stars shine with their own innate and proper Light.
2. That the Moon and other Planets in our System have no light of their own, but receive it of the Sun.
3. That the Earth differs no (ratione luminu) in respect of her light, from the other Planets.
4. That the Sun may be numbred [sic] among the Fixed Stars, and the Earth among the Planets. . . .
6. That the Fixed Stars are far remote, and without the Perimeter of the Sphere of Saturn, yet are not (as Antiquity thought) all plac'd in one Sphere, but every one hath a vast space about it (perhaps a plenary System) destitute of other Fixed Stars.
7. That the Heavens have Fluid and not Solid Orbs.
8. That the Earth resteth in its Sphere, or Heaven, yet notwithstanding is carried about by virtue thereof, which may also be understood of all the other Planets.
9. That the Earth (speaking properly) is not moved nor any of the other Planets, altho' they are transferr'd or carried about by their Orb or Heaven.
10. That all the Primary Planets are carried about the Sun, who is the true and undoubted Center of their Vortex.
11. That as the Earth is carried about the Sun as her proper Center, even so is the Moon Transferr'd about the Earth.
12. That all the Planets are not carried about the Sun in perfect Circles, but in Elliptick Paths or Orbs.
13. That no Translation of the Earth, can cause any Parallax in the Fixed Stars, in respect of their great distance from the Eye.
14. That it is altogether impossible to know the Distance of the Fixed Stars from the Earth, and consequently from one another.

15. That if the Earth were beheld from Saturn, it would appear much like to him both in Magnitude and Lustre.

16. That the Direction, Retrogradiations, and Stations of the Planets, with the Velocity and Tardity of their Motions, are not Essential but only an appearance at the Earth in respect of their Situation and Position, one to another.

17. That the Distance of the Planets, may be known both from the Earth and from the Sun, and mutually from one another.

18. That the Secondary Planets (as the Moon and the Circumjovials) are carried about their Primary Planets, and retain their Bodies for their Centers, about which they move.

19. That the Earth (and probably the other Planets) hath a proper Motion upon her own Axis, which is uniform, equal, in respect of the Conversions of her Meridian to the Sun.

20. That all the Phaenomena of the Heavens may (upon the Copernican System) most easily and exactly be resolved and determined according to these Principles.

12. As with the other almanacs, regardless of the position on judicial astrology, current scientific knowledge demanded reverence in *Culpepper Revived*: "Wonderful Glorious, and Marvellous are the Works of the Infinite God which are, in part, to be sought out by them that have Pleasure therein. . . . And who is it that can, or dare deny God's Government of the World by Angels and Stars, for his Angels are his Ministring Spirits, and (as one observes) the Stars his Militia; for the Stars in their Courses fought against Sisera." Perhaps the key to this outlook was the phrase "in part." The assumption that empirical study can yield total knowledge has, of course, an outlook fundamentally different from one that consciously knows "in part." If the former belief is fairly widespread today, one ought to be cautious in ascribing it to people in the past.

13. *Fly's* terms are typical: "belly . . . loins . . . reins . . . secret member and bladder . . . hips . . . thighs . . . knees . . . hams . . . legs and ancles [sic] . . . feet . . . toes . . . head and face . . . neck . . . throat . . . arms and shoulders . . . breast . . . stomach . . . heart . . . back, [or] bowels." Or as *Culpepper Revived* would have it: "belly . . . reins . . . loins . . . secrets . . . thighs . . . knees . . . legs . . . feet . . . head . . . face . . . neck . . . throat . . . arms . . . shoulders . . . brest . . . stomach . . . heart . . . back . . . [or] bowel."

If we see the human body mainly in terms of systems, they saw it in terms of parts. Our view is primarily functional; theirs was positional. The implications of such an understanding for social and personal perceptions could be significant. A positional conception of the body necessarily highlights appearance—wholeness, symmetry, texture, motion, and color—over performance in judging health, ability, and maintenance. Viewed in this light, the physical person becomes almost entirely symbolic. Self becomes a matter of presentation more than ability, of image more than production. Would it be stretching the evidence too far, then, to suppose that the eighteenth century obsession with social category—with the "quality" of individual persons—reflects this particular conception of the material human being? Was a functional view of the body a prerequisite to an egalitarian social ethic?

14. Franklin, *Poor Richard: The Almanacks for the Years 1733–1758*, 5.

15. Curry, 11. For a convincing argument that this cosmology was prevalent in Britain well beyond the early eighteenth century, see Wiggins. *Prophecy and Power*, 11.

16. Capp, *English Almanacs*, 385.

17. Colin Kidd, *British Identities before Nationalism: Ethnicity and Nationhood in the Atlantic World, 1600–1800* (Cambridge: Cambridge University Press, 1999), 10.

18. Colley, 73–77. Wing, *Olympia Domata*.

19. Linda Colley, *Britons: Forging the Nation 1707–1837* (New Haven: Yale University Press, 1992), 73–77.

20. I risk implying, in this brief verbal gesture, that only anti-Jacobites favored order, stability and survival. Anti-Jacobites such as the Stationers would surely have seen the matter this way, but Paul Monod reminds us that the problem of instability and disunity was a fundamental preoccupation on all portions of the political spectrum in eighteenth-century Britain—Jacobite, Tory and Whig alike. His model of an eighteenth-century British polity shaped less by oligarchic stability than by "dynamic tension" between competing mythologies of order is particularly compelling. See *Jacobitism and the English Peoople, 1688–788* (Cambridge: Cambridge UP, 1989) 349.

ᘒ Chapter Eight ᘒ

Conclusion

*I*t comes as no surprise to find an entire annual run of eighteenth-century English almanacs containing a unified social and political message. Except for piracies (and this may have been a very large exception indeed), these almanacs had one author: the Stationers' Company itself. As literary commodities, they were designed to sell, and as Company products they were designed to promote a specific public image of the guild. Despite their apparent variety, then, these almanacs contained a message which conformed both to the demands of the almanac market and to the values and interests of the Company. One expects that further study will note variations in the Stationer almanacs' message over the course of the eighteenth century.[1] But this study suggests that such variations must have reflected changes in the relationship between consumer tastes, Company interests, the English Stock monopoly and national politics.[2]

Taken as a whole, the stationers' political-religious loyalties in the early eighteenth century inclined toward the status quo in its most tolerant and stable form. This was consistent with the Company's primary public interest: the preservation of its English Stock monopoly. That coincidence need not raise questions of sincerity. In every way imaginable, stability, loyalty and unity were in the Company's interest. Its members had strong personal and collective motives to minimize disagreement and emphasize inclusiveness. Upheaval and rebellion were simply not good for health or for business, and of course, the lucrative English Stock monopoly depended on the continued favor of the current government. This spectrum of interests, and particularly the monopoly, linked the Company's interests inextricably with those of the government. The Stamp Act of 1711 only served to cement this connection. Broad-minded latitudinarianism, theologically permissive and morally

earnest, appealed to leading stationers for the same reason it appealed
to Robert Walpole. A latitudinarian society privileged inclusion and order over radical idealism; it was the classic recipe for stability.[3] Small
wonder that the Company almanacs pled for unity, order and loyalty,
and castigated all threats to stability, regardless of party or nationality.

When it made decisions about who received Company patronage,
the Court of Assistants did not consciously consider how its choices affected the content of Company almanacs. Its fundamental concern when
handing out jobs was the good of the Company and the welfare of its
constituents. Yet the apparent lack of connection between almanac printers and almanac content may be deceptive. It was no accident that the
stationers' almanacs championed the same values that guided its patronage: an urgent preoccupation with practical outcome, a commitment to
tangible benefit, and quest to extend and secure social cohesion. The
Company's tacit code for internal piracy exemplified this esteem for com-
promise and pragmatic accommodation, and the stationers' almanacs
championed the same virtues. The almanacs lauded those who, like assistants doling out patronage, were willing to work with imperfect resources to achieve the greatest possible good. Also, perhaps with Benjamin
Harris in mind, they condemned any whose self-defined benefit would
result in wider social harm. The English almanacs for 1712 took, in a
word, quite a stationer-esque view of things.

English almanacs, then, were the product of a dynamic interplay
between the demands of the market and the desires of the ruling order.
Eighteenth-century England was remarkable for an extensive confluence
of those impulses, and for the general social and political stability that
resulted from it. The millions of almanacs consumed during the same era
reflected that confluence. Yet the possibility also remains that those almanacs—the most widely read literature after Bibles and newspapers—
influenced this trend even as they reflected it. With their commitment
to the propaganda of stability and cohesion, the stationers' exclusive
right to almanac authorship may have been one of the major forces
shaping public attitudes in early eighteenth-century Britain.

Notes

1. A thematic survey of one almanac title over the course of the century indicates that while variations exist, they occurred within narrow boundaries.
Moore's *Vox Stellarum* appealed to "the solid sober, and sensible part of
mankind" not only in 1711 but throughout the eighteenth century. It consistently reflected "the wish of many British subjects to defend the existing politi-

cal order, especially when it was under threat" and the view of many common folk "that the aristocratic constitution of Britain provided them and the country at large with many benefits and advantages." Loyalty to the crown irrespective of party "had long played a major role in Moore's message," and this was never more true than in the last years of Anne's reign: "When in 1710 the Sacheverell crisis increased concern about the true Church of England and raised the issue of national war-weariness, Moore turned his comments towards a desire for peace . . . Moore's initial support for the war, for Marlborough and for the position of the Whigs turned into an acclamation for the Tory peace." Wiggins, 118–123.

2. It would be particularly interesting to determine how—or whether—almanac content changed after 1775, when the dissolution of the monopoly severed the direct link between Company interests and government approval.

3. Readers of John Grenville Agard Pocock will recognize this sentiment as an undifferentiated expression of the ideology of "commerce" whose interplay with the "virtue" of classical republicanism comprises a guiding theme of that eminent scholar's corpus. This paper implies that a study of the extent and nature of commercial and republican notions among the less articulate members of early modern British society might supplement the erudite work Professor Pocock continues to do with the theorists of the day.

Index

www.ingramcontent.com/pod-product-compliance
Lightning Source LLC
Chambersburg PA
CBHW080928100426
42812CB00007B/2405